WHAT WOULD
REAGAN DO?

Life Lessons from the Last Great President

CHRIS CHRISTIE

WITH ELLIS HENICAN

THRESHOLD EDITIONS

New York   Amsterdam/Antwerp   London   Toronto   Sydney   New Delhi

Threshold Editions
An Imprint of Simon & Schuster, LLC
1230 Avenue of the Americas
New York, NY 10020

First Threshold Editions trade paperback edition January 2025

THRESHOLD EDITIONS and colophon are
trademarks of Simon & Schuster, LLC

For information about special discounts for bulk purchases,
please contact Simon & Schuster Special Sales at
1-866-506-1949 or business@simonandschuster.com.

The Simon & Schuster Speakers Bureau can bring authors to your live event. For more information, or to book an event, contact the Simon & Schuster Speakers Bureau at 1-866-248-3049 or visit our website at www.simonspeakers.com.

Interior design by Jaime Putorti

Manufactured in the United States of America

10 9 8 7 6 5 4 3 2 1

Library of Congress Cataloging-in-Publication Data

ISBN 978-1-9821-6066-1
ISBN 978-1-9821-6067-8 (pbk)
ISBN 978-1-9821-6068-5 (ebook)

This book is dedicated to my wife and lifelong partner, Mary Pat, the person who has always believed in me and shared with me our faith in our family, our country, and our responsibility to try to make both the best they can be.

CONTENTS

WHAT WOULD
REAGAN DO?

INTRODUCTION

FIRST TIME

You never forget the first time.

Freshman year. University of Delaware. I was finally out of my parents' house and trying to turn a cramped dorm room double—outfitted to hold three of us—into a place of my own. That took some ingenuity when the chief design feature was a trio of stiff metal twin beds with thin, creaky mattresses, longer but no wider or any more comfortable than army cots.

Welcome to college life, young man.

I turned eighteen that September, which still didn't make me legal at the Deer Park Tavern or the Stone Balloon or Klondike Kate's. The drinking age in Delaware was twenty at the time, though I have to say I don't remember much carding at any of the bars near campus. But I'd be old enough to vote in the November election, and I damn sure wasn't going to miss what felt to me that fall like a golden opportunity.

I was definitely more conservative than some of my new classmates, many of whom seemed to think that nuclear power was a dire threat to the planet and that Big Business loved nothing more than dumping pollution into the rivers and streams. But I'd been class president all four years at Livingston High in New Jersey, and I hoped to get active in student government at Delaware. I was always up for a spirited debate. I already knew I'd be majoring in political science. I remembered four years earlier, in the summer between eighth and ninth grades, sitting at home with my parents and watching every night of the Democratic convention from Madison Square Garden as an obscure governor from Georgia named Jimmy Carter nailed down the nomination against a big field of higher-profile Washington types. Then it was the Republicans' turn in Kansas City. Former California governor Ronald Reagan almost snatched his party's nomination from Gerald Ford, who had become president after Richard Nixon resigned because of Watergate.

The soaring oratory, the backroom deals, the floor reporters jamming microphones into the faces of delegates from all over the country—every action-packed minute of it made me think: *This is so cool. . . .*

The last night of the Republican convention, after Ford had already accepted the nomination, they called Reagan back to the podium. He delivered a speech filled with so much passion and optimism, it almost sounded like Reagan, not Ford, was the candidate who'd won. "I believe the Republican Party has a platform that is a banner of bold, unmistakable colors with no pale, pastel shades," Reagan told the spellbound delegates. What the Democrats were offering, he said, was "nothing but a revamp and a reissue and a rerunning of a late, late show of the thing that we have been hearing from them for the last forty years."

My father pointed out that Reagan's speech hadn't exactly endorsed Ford. But the former California governor's stirring words and his natural delivery made voting for a Republican sound exciting and something to be proud of, like a team you'd want to play on. I could tell Reagan had the whole convention hall right in the palm of his hands. It was just after Reagan finished that I turned to my parents, who were sitting next to each other on the couch, and announced to them:

"I'm a Republican."

To me, the Republicans seemed to put their faith in people, while the Democrats believed most of all in government. It was a simple distinction but, to me, a very big one.

So here I was, four years later, finally old enough to vote. By then Gerald Ford was ancient news, having lost to Jimmy Carter. Ronald Reagan, who'd made such an impression on me and a lot of other people the last time around, was now the 1980 Republican presidential nominee. This time, he'd cruised past a lineup of other Republican hopefuls, including former CIA director George Bush, who had now joined the ticket as Reagan's running mate. Carter was back, asking for a second term.

To eighteen-year-old me, the choice was obvious. Carter seemed like a nice enough man, but he clearly wasn't up to the job of president. My high school years had been filled with bad news from Washington. The economy was tanking. Prices kept going up. For a while there, you could buy gas only on certain days of the week, and they kept messing around with daylight saving time. All around the world, America was coming up short. The Soviet Union kept causing trouble, doing things like invading Afghanistan, which provoked a boycott by the United States of the 1980 Olympics. But the worst of it might have been Iran, where a militant gang of heavily armed students were holding fifty-two American hostages and refusing to let them go. Clearly, the University of Tehran had some extracurricular groups we didn't have at Delaware. And President Carter didn't have a clue what to do about it.

Reagan was different. Very different. For one thing, he seemed focused and confident. He also knew what he stood for and he laid it all out. He wanted to cut taxes, make the economy stronger, let America produce more of its own energy, and not take any crap from our enemies. That all sounded good to me. Unlike Carter, who mumbled and meandered, Reagan could express all this clearly and eloquently in a way that a lot of people could relate to . . . and not just conservatives. He was one of those politicians who, even if you disagreed with him, exuded a down-to-earth decency that made people think he was an OK guy. He'd been a governor and a movie star and the president of the actors' union in Hollywood. But he still seemed to grasp what real people were going through. The way he talked, he didn't seem to look down on anyone.

That first year in college, getting back and forth to New Jersey was a major hassle for me. I had my own car, a 1971 burnt-orange Camaro with a black vinyl roof—a great ride to have as a high school senior. But Delaware freshmen weren't allowed to keep a car on campus. So the Camaro sat in my parents' driveway. To get home, I had to board a bus in front of Rhodes Pharmacy near campus on

East Main Street and ride to the Port Authority Bus Terminal in New York City, then transfer to the DeCamp 77 bus to Livingston.

That could take *hours*.

So, as Election Day neared, I decided that my first vote for president was going to be absentee. It was a complicated process, more complicated than I imagined. First, I ordered an absentee ballot, and when it arrived, I sat at the plain wooden desk in my dorm room, 208 Harrington Hall E, and filled in the little box next to the Republican ticket, Reagan and Bush, and the seventeen electors who stood for them in New Jersey. I folded the sheet like the instruction said to, put it inside the security envelope, signed and dated the outside of the envelope, sealed the envelope, put that envelope into the prepaid return envelope, and finally dropped the package in the mail to the Essex County Board of Elections in New Jersey.

I was super careful. I didn't want to screw it up.

Once the ballot was in the mail, I felt like I had done something really important, like I really was on the way to being an adult. I was proud to be part of the presidential election, proud to help Ronald Reagan. I hoped we'd have a better country as a result.

My vote wasn't enough to deliver liberal Essex County. Carter was ahead there. But Reagan won New Jersey and its seventeen electoral votes, 1,546,557 to 1,147,364, and one of those Reagan votes was mine.

It wasn't a close election. Reagan swept into the White House in a forty-four-state landslide. A lot of people must have been feeling the same way I was. And given all the things that happened next, I have never regretted—not for one little second—the vote I cast from my dorm room that day.

I've voted hundreds of times since then, including several times for myself. That was exciting. But I have never been prouder about a vote than in the fall of 1980 when I cast that absentee ballot for Ronald Reagan.

Even now, I am still learning lessons from that man and the many examples he set for us. All of us can. He really did articulate what was special and powerful about America. To a remarkable degree, he turned his core conservative principles into reality and brought millions of new people into the cause while making our country a better place for everyone.

We have never needed Ronald Reagan more than we need him now.

The political life of America has grown so divisive, so hostile, and often so small, a lot of people can't even tell you anymore what they believe in. They just know that the other side is dead wrong.

No party has a monopoly on this ugly state of affairs. The Democrats have gone uber-progressive, catering to the endless demands of their party's far-left fringe, solving "problems" that aren't really problems while refusing to face catastrophes that very much are. I know that my mother, like a lot of people who used to identify as Democrats, would hardly recognize her old party anymore. At the same time, too many Republicans have abandoned their common sense and discernment and jumped into a shabby cult, denying plain reality, ignoring proven facts, promoting ridiculous conspiracies, and pledging allegiance to a blustery loser who can't remotely be called a conservative and cares solely about himself.

That's a recipe for electoral defeat if I've ever heard one—if not a road to total political collapse. It's making the Republican tent smaller, not larger. It's about as far as you can get from Ronald Reagan.

It's a shame we've reached the point where we have to do this . . . but we need to learn the powerful lessons of Reagan all over again.

In the pages that follow, I will dive into some of the most dramatic and revealing moments of Reagan's life and career, watching how he handled challenging situations, exploring the strategies he employed, and observing the relationships he nurtured, often across the political spectrum and the international divide. And I will share my unique insights on all of it. It's amazing how much Reagan was able to achieve by sticking to his principles and connecting on a human level with those around him. It's been two decades since Reagan left us, and yet many of his leadership lessons are directly relevant to the greatest challenges we face today.

Many times, I have asked myself, *What would Reagan do?* Here's my chance to explore that with you in an intimate way. In this history, I'm convinced we can find solutions to some of the largest challenges of today.

Each chapter of this book is not only great history, it also contains a blueprint for bringing our country back to achieving big things at home and around the world. It's amazing the insights we can gather if we simply pause to ask: What would Reagan do?

CHAPTER 1

JACK AND NELLE'S BOY

His father was a raging alcoholic. His mother was a living saint. And plopped between the two of them was the future fortieth president of the United States, trying to imagine a place for himself in a much larger world.

LESSON LEARNED: IF THE CHOICE COMES DOWN TO ANGER OR EMPATHY, GO WITH EMPATHY.

Even as a boy, when times were anything but easy, Ronald Reagan tended to look on the bright side. He had two parents who loved him, Jack and Nelle Reagan. The family always had food on the table and a roof over their heads, thanks almost entirely to the drive and persistence of his mother. The future president wasn't much of a student or the natural athlete his older brother, Neil, was. But he had his talents and his charms, and he would find his niche . . . *eventually*.

Over the years he would learn some hugely valuable lessons from his mother and father, their good and bad examples, and the quick succession of Depression-era towns the family called home.

About the importance of working hard. About the power of faith. About the need for empathy. *Especially* about empathy. Please don't be swept away by the gauzy recollections from those early years in northwestern Illinois that Reagan would polish up decades later for his popular banquet speeches and radio essays. His tumultuous upbringing also left him with an awful lot to overcome.

That's what happens when your father is a gregarious man but also a raging alcoholic who can't hold a job and erupts in sporadic fits of rage, while your mother toils day and night as a seamstress, holding the family together with grit, crossed fingers, and a deep reservoir of Christian faith. If you don't slide into bitterness or self-recrimination, you can actually learn some valuable lessons from a childhood like that.

Ronald Wilson Reagan, Jack and Nelle's second son, came into the world on February 6, 1911. Neil was two and a half years older. Both boys got early nicknames from their father, who had a quick wit and a knack for seeing the humor in things when he wasn't hungover or had something new to feel aggrieved about. Baby Ronald was Dutch because his father thought he looked like "a fat little Dutchman." The more boisterous Neil was Moon, after the *Moon Mullins* comic strip, which featured the antics of the lowbrow denizens of the Schmaltz boardinghouse.

Both names stuck.

The Reagans started out in a small, second-floor apartment in a brown-brick building on South Main Street in Tampico, Illinois (population 849), directly across from the H. C. Pitney Variety Store, where Jack worked on and off as a clerk and was certain he was underpaid. Chicago was 113 miles east, though it might as well have been a thousand. Davenport, Iowa, was much closer in the other direction . . . and not just in miles. This swampy patch of rural Illinois was drained when the mighty Chicago, Burlington and Quincy Railroad came through after the Civil War, though the economic boom promised by the CB&Q seemed to skip Tampico, especially the Reagan family, who barely had two nickels to rub together.

When the new baby was two months old, the Reagans moved to a ramshackle two-story rental on Glassburn Street near the rail depot on the outskirts of town. They stayed in that house until Pitney's closed in 1914, at which point they lived for brief stretches in Chicago, Galesburg (just as World War I was breaking out), and Monmouth, as Jack kept hunting for a better-paying job and nothing ever quite seemed to materialize. When Pitney's reopened in 1919, the Reagans returned briefly to Tampico, living in an apartment above the store. And all their moving around wasn't close to done. Once Pitney's closed again the following December, Jack moved the family forty miles east to the relative metropolis of Dixon (population 8,191) and a cedar-shingled, gable-roofed Queen Anne on South Hennepin Avenue, also a rental, that would later be known as "Ronald Reagan's Boyhood Home"—though it was, in fact, the *seventh* residence in the future president's first nine years. He and his brother shared one of the three bedrooms and slept in the same bed. The family remained there for barely two years, before moving again (to yet another "Ronald Reagan's Boyhood Home").

"I was forever the new kid in school," he would recall years later in his post-presidency memoir, *An American Life*, looking back on those dicey days of constantly being uprooted. During one four-year stretch, Dutch attended four different schools. He was the small boy at the bottom of the pile in pickup football games, the one constantly striking out on the baseball field. It didn't help that he was badly nearsighted and hated wearing glasses. He never forgot the sting of one missed fly ball in eighth grade. "Everybody was looking at me, expecting me to catch it. I just stood there. The ball landed behind me and everybody said, 'Oh, no!'" But new-boy jitters and flubbed fly balls weren't the only burdens borne by Jack Reagan's younger son. There was always the looming presence of Jack's first love.

Alcohol.

Though John Edward "Jack" Reagan had no more than a grade-school education, he was blessed with an innate likability and a quick turn of phrase. He was, everyone agreed, a natural salesman, thoroughly delightful to anyone who wasn't living with or counting on him. With his ready charm and friendly nature, Jack had no trouble landing jobs despite his spotty work record. His problem was *keeping* them. His fleeting job titles included clerk, store manager, and several kinds of traveling salesman, most often of shoes. And Jack liked to drink. *Really* liked to drink. He drank with such regularity and such gusto that he frequently had trouble getting up for work in the morning and staying focused during the day. By evening he was either roaring drunk or nearly comatose, depending on when you caught him. When he drank, he had a tendency to fly off the handle at his sons and his wife. Almost anything could set him off, as he was also burning through the patience of his latest employer and sending another wrecking ball through the family finances. Nelle took on extra sewing jobs to make ends meet. The boys kicked in from their after-school jobs. And soon the Reagans were filling out another change-of-address card at the post office.

Not all of this was Jack's fault. Good jobs were scarce those days in northwest Illinois. Many local farm families had lost their land to crushing debt. The big cement plant in Dixon had closed. At more and more of the downtown stores, the windows were covered with brown paper or plywood. But for the Reagans, Jack's drinking cast a shadow over *everything*, with all the frustration, embarrassment, and helplessness that implies. Along the way, Jack went on and off the wagon . . . and went on and fell off again. Promises made, promises broken, so often, who could possibly keep count? After a while, it wasn't that Jack tried and failed to give up drinking or struggled to get his life back on track. He mostly just quit trying, surrendering anew every day, and no one in the family held much hope that any of this would change.

So what could Jack Reagan's adolescent sons do about any of this? What could his long-suffering wife do? Not much. They could try to ignore the drinking. They could accept it as God's will. They could make excuses when he missed another family outing or made a scene at a weekend barbecue. And if they could summon enough courage and inner strength, they could make damn sure that Jack's weakness didn't drag the rest of the family down. In other words, they could learn.

For Dutch, there was one cold, blustery night, a night that would stick with him forever, a night no child should ever have to endure. He'd just come home from the YMCA. His mother was out somewhere on a sewing job. He assumed the house would be empty. But just before he reached the front door, he tripped over a lump he didn't know was there. It was Jack, flat on his back, sprawled out in the snow.

"I leaned over to see what was wrong and smelled whiskey," Reagan wrote in his memoir, remembering the scene like it was yesterday. "He had found his way home from a speakeasy and had just passed out right there." For a moment, Dutch looked down and thought about going inside and trying to forget what he'd just seen. But he couldn't do it. "When I tried to wake him he just snored— loud enough, I suspected, for the whole neighborhood to hear." Instead, the boy grabbed a handful of his father's overcoat, gave it a stiff yank, and dragged Jack into the house. He put his father to bed and never breathed a word about any of it to his mother.

No doubt, Nelle would have been pained to hear it. But it's hard to imagine she would have been surprised. Having a drunk in the family can make you angry and bitter. Or it can make you empathize. Though young Dutch struggled sometimes to get there, he landed on the compassionate side, thanks mostly to his mom.

Nelle Wilson Reagan was the kind of woman who took care of business without ever allowing herself to feel discouraged or wasting a dime. She mended Moon's dress slacks so they could be handed down to Dutch. She served oatmeal with gravy and made it sound like a delicacy. She could make a soup bone last a week. Then she'd take on yet another sewing job. Given her husband's shaky performance as a breadwinner, what choice did she have? She needed to keep her boys moving forward and her family out of the poorhouse. And much of her strength seemed to come from above.

Though Jack could politely be called a "cultural Catholic"—more team spirit than churchly devotion—Nelle lived her religion every day. She was a dedicated worshipper at the First Christian Church (Disciples of Christ), a rugged Protestant denomination that sprang up in the mid-1800s on the American frontier. She gave Bible readings to the congregation. She taught Sunday school. A strong believer in the power of divine intervention, she led the midweek prayer group when the pastor was away. Hers was a stubbornly optimistic Christianity, morally certain that a mixture of hard work and God-given goodness was a reliable route to success in life, no matter what life threw your way. That was the practical faith that Nelle Reagan passed on to her younger son, and it helped define the man he would become. Without it, there would be no smiling, cheerful candidate on all those campaign posters and commercials so many decades later, no happy warrior staring down Tip O'Neill and Mikhail Gorbachev. Nelle's optimism stood out even more in comparison to Jack's chronic failure to detox and provide for his family. As her younger son would put it years later, she "always expected to find the best in people and often did."

Dutch never embraced the churchly devotion that his mother displayed. He believed in a higher power and went to services on Sunday without ever centering his life around the rituals of organized religion as his mother so dedicatedly did. He had a faith that was open and welcoming and, in later years, would be easy for others to relate to even though there was no way he could truly be called devout. But at age ten Dutch chose to be baptized at his mother's First Christian Church on Dixon's South Hennepin Avenue, even though his older brother had already followed their father into Catholicism—or Jack's version of it, anyway.

One thing Nelle never did around the boys was blame Jack for his boozing, even when he'd spent the previous night drunkenly raging around the house. "Nelle tried so hard to make it clear he had a sickness that he couldn't help, and she constantly reminded us of how good he was to us when he wasn't drinking," his younger son recalled. This was a highly progressive view for its time. Many people, including many devout Christians, would have seen Jack's alcoholism as a moral failing, a character flaw or the kind of sin that could very well consign him to an eternity at Satan's subterranean, round-the-clock barbecue. Nelle wasn't so judgmental. Not in that way. Instead of running down her husband, she helped her boys find reasons to admire him, including his strong aversion to racial and religious bigotry. In later years, Ronald Reagan's political enemies would denounce him as a racist who cruelly stripped the poor of much-needed benefits. In fact, from his own family's struggles, he had a keen understanding that people needed a hand sometimes. From his father especially, he got a strong conviction that prejudice of any kind was unacceptable. That's how Dutch and Moon were raised. They spent their childhoods playing outside with white *and* *Black* children. The boys were urged to invite their classmates home for supper, regardless of race or religion, and to treat all people the same. As Ronald Reagan would put it later: "There was no more grievous sin at our household than a racial slur."

* * *

Though he got into his share of small-town scrapes, young Dutch mostly dodged serious trouble—like the time he was messing around in a train yard and one of the trains started moving with him underneath. That was a close call! But credit a spark of sibling rivalry for igniting the passion that would become his adult career.

Nelle, who'd always been a bit of a ham, began organizing amateur performances at her church. Members of the congregation, young and old, chose selections from poems, speeches, plays, and books and then recited them from memory. Older son Neil, who was game for most things, stepped right up when his mother asked. But the shyer Dutch? He was a harder sell. Though he often attended services with his mother, he wasn't so sure he wanted to stand up in front of all those people. What if he got up there and forgot his lines? But when he saw Neil performing and seeming to have a good time . . . well, the sibling rivalry kicked in, and he told his mother he would give it a try.

"Summoning my courage, I walked up to the stage that night, cleared my throat, and made my theatrical debut," he reported. "I don't remember what I said, but I'll never forget the response: People laughed and applauded."

That was something new for the reserved, nearsighted C student who'd moved from town to town and wasn't much of an athlete and sometimes felt like he lived in his brother's shadow. Suddenly, even Jack's drinking seemed a million miles away. "I liked it," Reagan said of his maiden performance and the response he got. "For a kid suffering childhood pangs of insecurity, the applause was music."

You can draw a straight line from that night in Dixon to Hollywood, Sacramento, and Washington. Not a short line, but a straight one. And B. J. Fraser definitely helped things along. He was the new sophomore English teacher at Dixon North High. "Young, self-possessed with a quiet and wry sense of humor, he seemed to open new doors that made learning an adventure," as Reagan would later describe him in a favorite-teacher essay for the *Washington Post*. "B.J. taught English but the emphasis wasn't on punctuation and sentence structure. Oh, he didn't sluff that off but you discovered he was more interested in originality. He taught us how to think, not what to think."

It so happened that Mr. Fraser was also the head of the drama club. He led the students in Broadway-style productions like Philip Barry's *You and I*, where the future president had his first stage performance outside church. "He opened the door on a world we'd never thought about before . . . ," Reagan said. By then, the young man clearly had the performance bug. "For a teenager still carrying around some old feelings of insecurity, the reaction of my classmates was more music to my ears," he remembered. "The experience grew more habit-forming with each curtain call. By the time I was a senior, I was so addicted to student theatrical productions that you couldn't keep me out of them."

It's always a crapshoot trying to pinpoint the influence that other people have on someone else's life. How much is nature? How much is nurture? How many of our talents are God-given and how many are learned? How much of what we achieve in life is total luck? It's always a mishmash. So it was with the young Ronald Reagan.

As he moved toward adulthood, Dutch definitely grew more confident. He eventually made the football team as a lineman, a position that didn't require too much speed or agility, just a refusal to budge. He was elected to various positions on the Dixon North student council, his first taste of public office. And he excelled as a Lowell Park lifeguard on the treacherous Rock River, a job that gave him a certain amount of teenage cool, even with the onesie swimwear that was standard male attire at the time. He would eventually be credited with saving seventy-seven people from drowning—surely an exaggeration, but still . . .

Though Dutch Reagan was influenced by many people, as all of us are, no three people had greater impact on the formation of the future president than Jack Reagan, Nelle Reagan, and B. J. Fraser—in their completely different ways.

From his father's struggles with the bottle and his shaky employment endeavors, Dutch learned how challenging life can be for ordinary people and the duty that all of us carry to show compassion and empathy. Jack's obvious failings could easily have saddled his son with a lifetime of resentment and bitterness. Instead, with Nelle's firm guidance and his own innate cheerful nature, the experience magnified Dutch's sense of social responsibility, something he would carry with him forever, even as his politics grew more conservative over the years.

From his mother's clear example, the future president learned about the power of hard work and persistence, especially when coupled with faith. Like her children, only more so, Nelle had every reason to feel aggrieved by the hand that life had dealt her. She, too, could have spent decades pointing fingers, casting blame, and cursing the heavens for her undeserved fate. But she never buckled under the harsh circumstances. Instead, she got busy, and she stayed that way. As a fill-in breadwinner. As an inspiring role model to her family and her community. As a beacon of moral clarity in a family that today would be declared *obviously dysfunctional.* With Nelle in charge, the Reagan home did the job it was meant to, sending two strong boys out into the world with the tools to succeed. She picked up the slack without complaining. She made sure her sons absorbed the lessons that would carry them into the future, avoiding a wide array of easy pitfalls.

No, never underestimate the influence of a strong mother's love.

And thanks to an inspiring English teacher and drama club director, the young Ronald Reagan was set on a path he would follow for the rest of his life. B. J. Fraser didn't have the influence on the insecure teenager that either of his parents did. No one could, and Mr. Fraser wasn't around nearly as long. But he played an indispensable role in defining what lay ahead, a truly remarkable journey out of Illinois that would include a three-decade career in Hollywood, two terms as the governor of California, and a vaunted place in history as one of America's most consequential and effective presidents. A big part of that flowed from Reagan's ability to present himself, to connect with ordinary people, to stand in front of a crowd and communicate. Were it not for B. J. Fraser, the Great Communicator of the Twentieth Century might never have taken that remarkable talent out of a certain Disciples of Christ church on South Hennepin Avenue in Dixon, Illinois.

All these experiences helped to make Ronald Reagan the leader he would become. Big-hearted. Inspirational. Principled. The happy storyteller who was also a sharp-eyed realist. He had a childhood filled with challenges and confusion across a background of Midwest simplicity, and it didn't destroy him. Instead, it taught him that challenges were real but surmountable with hard work, clear vision, and the help of others. It developed in him a steel spine and a cushion of empathy. "As I look back on those days in Dixon," he would write many years later, "I think my life was as sweet and idyllic as it could be, as close as I could imagine for a young boy to the world created by Mark Twain in *The Adventures of Tom Sawyer.*"

Reagan's early years were, if anything, several shades darker than that of the good-hearted mischief-maker Tom. But the simple fact that he could recall his childhood so warmly and pronounce it such a triumph—that was an early victory right there.

CHAPTER 2

INSPIRED FOR LIFE

As his first political hero, Reagan chose the father of the New Deal, whose big-government solutions he would later seek to dismantle. But Reagan would never lose his love for Franklin Roosevelt, and Roosevelt's core values would never abandon him.

LESSON LEARNED: POLITICS CAN CHANGE.
CHARACTER IS FOREVER.

Ronald Reagan cast his first vote for president on November 8, 1932, nine months and two days after his twenty-first birthday. On that bright fall morning, he helped the Democratic challenger, Franklin Delano Roosevelt, trounce Herbert Hoover, the incumbent Republican. America, which was having all kinds of troubles, got a bold new direction that day.

Reagan was five months out of Eureka College, a small Christian school affiliated with the Disciples of Christ, where he lettered in football, track, and swimming, acted in student plays, pledged the Tau Kappa Epsilon fraternity, joined the debate club, worked as a reporter on the school newspaper, helped edit the yearbook, served as president of the student council, and earned a bachelor's degree in economics and sociology. No, you couldn't call him shy or awkward anymore. And he did all that while also holding down part-time jobs as a lifeguard, assistant swim coach, and girl's-dorm dishwasher to help pay his tuition and send a few bucks home to his struggling parents in Dixon, ninety miles north. Despite all that, or maybe because of his exuberance for college life, he was still a C student. He still went by "Dutch," his childhood nickname. But whatever personal reticence he had in high school, he'd clearly shaken off by then.

He might have been best known on campus for making a stirring speech on behalf of his fellow students who were striking to restore classes the administration had cut because of financial strains from the Great Depression. After the strike, the college president resigned.

"Everything that has been good in my life began here," he would declare at the Eureka College commencement exactly fifty years after his own graduation. A gracious exaggeration, perhaps, but a lot of good things had happened to him by then, including being elected president. Still, Reagan could hardly have chosen a worse time to come out of college and try to launch a career.

The nation was three years into the Depression. One in four American adults had no work, more than 15 million people. Breadlines and soup kitchens were a daily necessity. Things were especially bleak in places like rural Illinois, where every farm failure meant another family had just lost its land and the stores in town had just lost another customer or supplier. Hardworking, well-rooted people were suddenly packing their cars—or, in more dire cases, hopping the rails—and heading off to Chicago, Cleveland, California, or someplace else they figured they might as well try their luck.

Dutch had a terrible time finding steady work, even with his shiny new college degree. He was living back at home in Dixon, going off on interviews and picking up odd jobs. Since it was summer, he signed up for lifeguarding again (for the seventh and, he hoped, final time). And he joined his mom and dad as a volunteer on the Roosevelt-for-president campaign, ringing doorbells and dropping palm cards on porches when the people weren't home. Unlike most people in Dixon, both his parents were reliable Democrats, though his father was far more outspoken about politics than his mother was. She was too busy working. But all the Reagans were firmly in the camp of the energetic challenger over the worn-out incumbent, whose answer for the tough times of the Depression seemed to be "More of the same." Herbert Hoover certainly gave Jack Reagan plenty to grouse about, with or without a beer in his hand. It wasn't like the Reagans ever had a big cushion in their lives, even in good times. And these certainly weren't those.

By fall, Dutch had finally landed a job, though it didn't sound like much of a prize: a temporary position as a sports broadcaster and general announcer at WOC, a tiny radio station just across the Iowa line in Davenport. There was nothing glamorous about the station whose call letters stood for World of Chiropractic. Ten dollars a game plus bus fare. That sounded fine: no more hitchhiking or borrowing the family's Oldsmobile. He took a small room at the Kimball House Hotel on East Fourth Street and hoped for the best. He did *love* sports. Everyone agreed he could talk. Hadn't he proven that on the college debate team and the student council? And as he made his first steps into adulthood, he was still very much his mother's son. Working hard. Always making himself available. Eager to leave a good impression. By this point he'd also absorbed a dose of his father's charm—thankfully, without Jack Reagan's self-destructive habits. And when Election Day arrived that year, right in the middle of football season, the ballot he cast for Roosevelt was far more than a fleeting choice. In FDR, Dutch Reagan found his first political hero (just as I would find mine, decades later, in Ronald Reagan): a leader who seemed to care deeply about the plight of ordinary people, even though he'd come from a wealthy family. A politician who understood that many Americans needed a hand, as the Reagans certainly did. A national figure who got a young Ronald Reagan thinking about something he had never considered before.

"All across the nation, millions of new voters looked at this President who was filled with confidence in the future, faith in the people, and the joy of the democratic rough-and-tumble, and they said to themselves maybe someday they, too, would like to serve the Nation in public life," Reagan would recall at the National Archives many years later at an event honoring the Franklin D. Roosevelt Library. That feeling was still fresh in his mind. "I was one of those millions," he said.

He didn't do anything about it right away. Not for a long while. But that first vote sealed Ronald Reagan's lifelong admiration for the big-government Democrat who would soon become known as the father of Social Security, the federal minimum wage, union expansion, tightened banking regulation, massive public works projects, and a wide array of family-benefit programs that, taken all together, would come to be known as the New Deal.

Did I say *lifelong*? Yes, lifelong. That's what so interesting. Reagan's political outlook would shift dramatically in the decades to come as he migrated from big-government, social-welfare Democrat to small-government, fiscally conservative Republican. But he would never for a minute try to hide the esteem—*awe*, even—that he felt for Franklin Delano Roosevelt. Forget about party labels! That would stick with Reagan forever. Even in the Oval Office, he would sometimes recite lines from Roosevelt's speeches that he had committed to memory, leaving Republican staffers and White House aides shaking their heads. But they could all see how influential Roosevelt had been to him and continued to be.

To many Republicans, myself included, Reagan would come to exemplify the core values and instincts of the Republican Party— what those values and instincts *ought to be*—and exemplify them better than anyone else was able to. Yet it was clear to those who knew Reagan best that he saw FDR as a personal role model long after their politics had diverged.

The renowned historian David McCullough said that of all the presidents he had interviewed, Republicans and Democrats, none had spoken with more enthusiasm for Roosevelt than Reagan had. When McCullough asked why, Reagan told him: "He never lost faith in this country for one minute," something that would often be said of Reagan over the years.

So, what could explain this unshakable bond? How could a small-government Republican like Reagan keep admiring a bureaucracy-bloating Democrat like Roosevelt, even as Reagan moved sharply to the right and dedicated himself to dismantling parts of the welfare state that Roosevelt had worked so hard to build?

Well, Roosevelt's faith in ordinary people clearly had something to do with it, as Reagan explained in his National Archives speech. But it was more than that. For Reagan, Roosevelt was personal, and it went back to the younger man's early adulthood. In Roosevelt, the budding radio announcer and future president saw something he hoped to emulate and would spend a lifetime pursuing. Something worth believing in. Something worth learning from. Character, it was called, and for Reagan it was larger than politics.

There is no doubt in my mind that Reagan would be appalled today by the lack of character on both sides of the aisle. From Eric Holder to Adam Schiff, from George Santos to Jared Kushner, the greed, dishonesty, naked ambition, and lack of truth from today's public officials would anger Reagan. Donald Trump is used by all of these folks as either an inspiration or an excuse for a lack of character. But Reagan would quickly reject that pervasive tendency for what it is: using the awful character of another leader to justify moral failings of their own. Reagan inspired more. Reagan demanded more. And because of it, he led a nation to greatness.

Franklin Roosevelt lived what he believed in. "The only thing we have to fear is fear itself," FDR told the nation in his 1933 inaugural address, as young Dutch was earning peanuts at WOC, covering basketball games in the 4,000-seat Davenport Central High gymnasium ("Go, Blue Devils!"). Roosevelt promised prompt, vigorous action and pleaded with Americans not to lose faith in themselves. All this struck a deep chord with Reagan. As he would put it later: "It was that ebullience, that infectious optimism, that made one young sportscaster think that maybe he should be more active as a citizen."

Among the people FDR's reforms directly benefited was Jack Reagan. As one of the few Democrats in his small corner of Illinois, Jack was rewarded for his activism by being named a local director of the Works Progress Administration, a key New Deal agency that ended up hiring 8.5 million people nationwide to build parks, roads, bridges, schools, libraries, armories, stadiums, swimming pools, and other public buildings and infrastructure: the Griffin Observatory in Los Angeles, the Hoover Dam in Nevada, Dealey Plaza in Dallas, the Atlantic City Reservoir in New Jersey, all the way down to the Canoe House at the University of Iowa. Big government doing big things, and the results were immediately visible. Two other New Deal programs, the Agricultural Adjustment Administration and the Farm Security Administration, eased rural poverty and saved countless family farms in places like northwestern Illinois. That in turn helped struggling Midwestern cities like Dixon, Davenport, and even tiny Tampico. No one had to explain to Ronald Reagan what Roosevelt's New Deal accomplished. He could see it with his own eyes, though in later years Reagan would often remind people that Roosevelt never expected the New Deal relief programs to be permanent. They would last only as long as they were needed, then shut down.

Well . . . that part didn't quite work out as planned.

When President Roosevelt swung through historically Republican Des Moines in 1936, Dutch got to witness the magic in person. He'd never seen anything like it before. "What a wave of affection and pride swept through that crowd as he passed by in an open car—a familiar smile on his lips, jaunty and confident, drawing from us a reservoir of confidence and enthusiasm some of us had forgotten we had in those days, those hard years. He really did convince us that the only thing we had to fear was . . . fear itself."

Over the years, Reagan would find many other things to admire about his political hero, even beyond Roosevelt's optimism and the impact of the New Deal. Some of it was stylistic. Some of it was much deeper than that. There was a lot in Roosevelt that Reagan would—you can't exactly call it *copy*, but things Reagan would learn from Roosevelt and eventually make his own.

Like Roosevelt's so-called fireside chats.

FDR had learned this trick when he was governor of New York. He was being pounded by Republicans in the legislature and by the Albany reporters who covered him. Instead of fighting with them to get his message out, he decided to go over their heads and speak directly to the people. His chosen method: live broadcasts on the Capital District's powerhouse WGY radio. As soon as he got to the White House, Roosevelt used the same technique on a national scale.

March 12, 1933. Eight days after his inauguration. Six days after shutting down the entire American banking system. He went on the radio with his first presidential fireside chat, telling the coast-to-coast Sunday night audience of more than 60 million people (just about half the entire country) "what has been done in the last few days, why it was done, and what the next steps are going to be."

That's how he spoke. Plainly and directly. And the nation—long before a partisan media would split the audience into fractions—tuned in to hear the president announce that a new program of federal deposit insurance would now allow the banks to open again.

Roosevelt wasn't actually in front of a fire. He sat at a desk with a microphone. But that didn't matter. No one could see him anyway. This was *radio*. What mattered, as Reagan well knew, was how you connected with the listeners and how you made them *feel*. Roosevelt was talking directly to the people, and they could tell he was speaking to them. Who needed a media middleman? Not a president with his own microphone. As a budding broadcaster himself, Reagan could recognize the power of that. *Speak to the people. Good news or bad news, they'd rather hear it from you. That's how leaders build credibility*. It was a lesson Reagan would never forget, right up through the frequent television addresses of his own presidency.

"To this day," Reagan marveled in *An American Life*, "no program in the history of radio has ever equaled the audience he had in his fireside chats." Because of Roosevelt's faith, Reagan added, "Our faith in our own capacity to overcome any crisis and any challenge was reborn."

That faith was not a religious faith. Not explicitly. It harkened back to the earliest days of America and what the nation stood for. "In this sense, FDR renewed the charter of the founders of our nation," Reagan said. "The founders had created a government of 'We the people.' Through a depression and a great war, crises that could well have led us in another direction, F.D.R. strengthened that charter. When others doubt, he said that we would find our salvation in our own hands—not in some elite but in ourselves. We'd find it where we'd always found it: in the towns, on the farms, in the stores and factories across America."

If that's not a summary of Reagan's future vision, I don't know what is.

When Japanese planes bombed the American naval base at Pearl Harbor, Roosevelt was just as explicit with the people he served. "Yesterday," he said, "December 7, 1941—a date which will live in infamy—the United States of America was suddenly and deliberately attacked by the naval and air forces of the Empire of Japan." And he kept talking to the nation as Germany and Italy declared war. Now, World War II was indeed a *world* war, and America was in it for real. Roosevelt fully understood what this would require: an enormous commitment from the people of America in blood, treasure, sweat, and tears. And he knew how to get it: by communicating directly with them.

The fireside chats continued. So did more formal addresses. In those years, nothing could stand between the people and their president. He kept communicating every step of the way. And Reagan never stopped listening.

With Roosevelt's leadership, millions of Americans served overseas in combat. Those who remained on the home front supported the war effort in every imaginable manner. Homemakers toiled in aircraft factories and munitions plants. People grew victory gardens, purchased Liberty Bonds, and rationed gasoline. Little children ate sugarless cereals and put margarine on their toast without complaining . . . make that, without complaining *too much*. However people were going to participate, first they had to believe.

Getting them there—that was Roosevelt's special gift, and Reagan could hardly turn his gaze away.

Reagan saw Roosevelt as a supremely transformative figure who revolutionized the government and its relationship to Americans. The fact that many of Reagan's fellow Republicans despised the New Deal, considering it corrosive to all things good about America, made no difference to Reagan. And there was one other reason Reagan held FDR in such high esteem: all along, the potent president who inspired so many was fighting a quiet battle of his own. A battle that was truly life-threatening. A battle that would become an increasing burden for him. It was the one thing Roosevelt hardly communicated at all.

It went all the way back to 1921, when Roosevelt was a thirty-nine-year-old lawyer in New York. He'd come down with a mystery illness. No one was quite sure what it was. But the symptoms included respiratory failure, urinary tract infections, painful ulcers, clots in his leg veins, malnutrition, and, most alarming of all, a worsening paralysis. Most of the symptoms resolved themselves, but he was left permanently paralyzed from the waist down.

Doctors at the time diagnosed the condition as a later-in-life case of infantile polio, though some medical experts now say it may have been a rare autoimmune disorder called Guillain-Barré syndrome. Whatever the cause, Roosevelt thought people would have a hard time accepting a leader who was physically disabled, especially in times like these.

So his public appearances were carefully choreographed. He used a wheelchair in private but never when cameras were around. Though he sometimes appeared on crutches, he insisted on being seen upright. Therefore, he often clung to the support of a family member or an aide. When making major speeches, he gripped a solid wooden lectern with both hands. Of course, he sat for his fireside chats, which may be one of the reasons he loved them so much.

It wasn't until March 1, 1945, about a month before he died, that Roosevelt fully referred in public to his disability. He spoke from his wheelchair that day, to Congress and to the American people of both parties, who'd stood by him for so long.

"I hope that you will pardon me for this unusual posture of sitting down," Roosevelt began, "but I know you will realize that it makes it a lot easier for me not to have to carry about ten pounds of steel around on the bottom of my legs."

That was it. He said it almost in passing. But anyone who'd been paying attention, as Ronald Reagan had, knew how monumental that was. And it only made Reagan admire the man even more. He revered Roosevelt's refusal to surrender to a crippling disease, regarding such perseverance as the noblest sort of achievement. Here was a man, regardless of political labels, who couldn't walk but had the strength and grace to help his country—Reagan's country—soar triumphantly at this time of existential need.

That was so much bigger than politics.

CHAPTER 3

TUNED IN

Without even realizing it, Reagan began learning the art of storytelling when he was a boy. But it was on the radio that he first became the Great Communicator.

LESSON LEARNED: FORGET ARGUMENTS AND STATISTICS. IF YOU REALLY WANT TO CONVINCE SOMEONE, TELL THEM A STORY.

His soothing baritone. His comfortable ad-libs. His ability to read a commercial and sound like he really loved the product. Especially that last one. They made Dutch Reagan a natural on the radio, and the listeners responded accordingly.

In November of 1933, with FDR safely in the White House, WOC Radio in Davenport merged with the much larger WHO Radio in Des Moines. Dutch's temporary job at the smaller station was ending. But management was so impressed with the young broadcaster's smooth delivery and his gift for staying cool under pressure that he was named chief sports announcer in Iowa's largest city, a full-time, permanent position. It was a big move up. WHO was an NBC Red Network affiliate with a blowtorch of a signal that lit up several Midwestern states every night when the sun went down, giving the twenty-two-year-old announcer a much wider audience. Even better, he'd be broadcasting the Chicago Cubs home games. Not from Wrigley Field. WHO didn't have that kind of budget. He would describe the action from messages on small slips of paper, typed by a telegraph operator who was transcribing plays sent by Morse code.

No more than rolling box scores. He couldn't see the games at all.

As the play-by-play man in Des Moines, it was Dutch's job to re-create the drama of every last pitch and at-bat for the local Cubs-mad audience, even though the radio studio was 333 miles from home plate. To make the action come alive, he had to reach into his own fertile imagination and flesh out the skeletal details.

If you think that's easy, I'll bet you've never tried it before.

There was one game that Reagan would never forget. June 7, 1934. The Cubs and the St. Louis Cardinals were 0–0 in the ninth inning. These were bitter National League rivals. Both teams were hot that year. Dizzy Dean, the brash right-hander on his way to thirty wins that season—and the pennant and World Series victory—was on the mound for the Cards. Billy Jurges, the Cubs' Bronx-born shortstop, was at the plate. At that crucial moment the telegraph line from Chicago went dead.

What happened next would become a staple of Ronald Reagan banquet speeches and keynote addresses for decades to come. As many times as he told it, he would always deliver the story with a twinkle in his eye.

"I saw my operator begin to type," he'd say.

So, I had the pitcher wind up and start his throw to the plate. Just then, I was handed the slip of paper, and it said: "The wire has gone dead." I had a ball on the way to the plate. The only thing I could think of that wouldn't get in the records was a foul ball. So, I had Jurges foul one down back of third base.

My operator shrugged and indicated he was getting no message from the ballpark.

There were several other stations broadcasting that game, and I knew I'd lose my audience if I told them we'd lost our telegraph connection. So, I took a chance. I had Jurges hit another foul. Then, I had him foul one that only missed being a home run by a foot. I had him foul one back in the stands and took up some time describing the two lads who got in a fight over the ball.

I kept on having him hit foul balls until I was setting a record for a ballplayer hitting successive foul balls, and I was getting more than a little scared. Just then, my operator started typing. When he passed me the paper, I started to giggle.

"Jurges popped out on the first ball pitched," it said.

Ugh! All those foul balls for nothing!

Who wouldn't get a kick out of a story like that?

As his audience smiled and shook their heads, half in admiration and half in disbelief, Reagan would confide: "I've waited a long time to tell that story. And I didn't tell it until after I was no longer a sports announcer."

At that point, the shaking heads would turn to nods. He had 'em. The audience was his.

As Reagan repeated that tale over the years, some of the details would change from time to time. In some renditions, he added the shouts of rowdy spectators or the sight of Cardinals manager Frankie Frisch marching out to the mound to calm the nerves of his jumpy pitcher, Dizzy Dean. Anything to burn up time. Sometimes he had a different pitcher on the mound or a different hitter at the plate. To Reagan, those details were trivial. They just didn't matter. What mattered was the *feeling* conveyed by the narrative, the boldness and the anxiety of a young radio announcer out on a limb, hanging on for dear life. A thoroughly familiar human emotion, experienced now in an exotic locale.

Who can't relate to that?

It wasn't only baseball. Reagan had a similar story that involved the Drake Relays, the nation's premier track-and-field event, which was held every April on the blue oval track at Drake University in Des Moines. As he kept being reminded on live radio, things didn't always go as planned.

"It happened ... in 1935," he told CBS sports broadcaster Vin Scully. "It was the day Jesse Owens broke three American records. Well, all day I'd been talking about the quarter mile, the 440. All day long, I had been telling the audience that this quarter mile was going to be the greatest event." But as race time neared, Drake University president Daniel Morehouse popped into the broadcasting booth to say a few words to the WHO audience. And a few more words. And a few more words after that. As the college president blabbered on, Reagan kept his eyes peeled on the blue oval below.

"And I sat there and listened to him speak into our microphone while I watched the quarter-mile event I'd been talking about all day," Reagan said. "When he signed off, I couldn't tell the audience it was all over so I just said, '[W]e're just in time for the event.' I got out my watch and knew it had to take about 48 seconds and I took them off and round the track and brought them in 1, 2, 3. There was no roar from the crowd so I explained that was because they were stunned by the sheer drama of the event."

In those days, Dutch Reagan and other sports announcers were constantly reporting events that had only the loosest connection to reality—and often no one was ever the wiser. Obviously, that would never fly today. But it was routine back then, flubs and all. Reagan told Vin Scully how one football announcer realized at the last moment that he had the wrong man running for a touchdown. The announcer wiggled out of it by saying, "Brown laterals to Smith, who scores."

Added Reagan: "The next spring, the famous Clem McCarthy called the wrong horse as the winner of the Preakness. Someone asked him, 'How could you call the wrong horse?' and he answered, 'Well, you can't lateral a horse.'"

Is it really such a leap from that kind of slipperiness to the fact-challenged art of political persuasion? Whether he knew it or not, Reagan had been training as an expert storyteller since he was a boy. From Jack's lubricated tales at the kitchen table to the high school debate team and the student council, all the way to FDR's fireside chats, hearing all those great stories, he couldn't help but grasp the enormous impact that a well-told story could have. Roosevelt needed to bring a nation together. Jack wanted to make people laugh. Both of them pulled you in gradually—not with arguments or facts or statistics but with tales of humanity. Seeing the world as it was, through real people's eyes.

Now that he was on the radio, it was Dutch's turn to shine.

In the years to come, Reagan's critics would be appalled by some of this. In those ancient radio broadcasts, they would hear purposeful deception. What he considered poetic license, they would call bogus falsehoods . . . or, today, *fake news*. In Reagan's day the naysayers would scour his speeches for the tiniest factual errors and howl, "Lies! Lies!" They wouldn't get the genius of the performance or the point of it all. But to Reagan the point of the story was always the point of the story. All that other stuff was just *there*. This is what one of Reagan's White House speechwriters was trying to get at—clumsily—by saying that Reagan spoke in "parables" and shouldn't be judged so harshly on the facts.

Just roll with it, in other words. You might even learn something.

Take a moment and think about what makes that Cubs foulball story work so well, why it's such a perfect *Ronald Reagan* story, and what it says about Reagan's extraordinary gift for reaching broad audiences and pulling them in. Truly, that one anecdote has everything that would come to exemplify the Reagan style of communication and, ultimately, get the future president crowned America's Great Communicator.

The story is easy to follow. It's funny in its absurdity. It has a clear point of view: that of a young sports announcer trying to get through a crisis without making a bad situation even worse. You don't need to be a rising broadcaster—or a baseball fan—to know how that feels.

The story takes listeners somewhere they normally don't get to go, behind the curtain of an earlier era in live sports radio. We are invited onto a terrain—the collision of sports and media—that lots of people are interested in. And the plot includes a bit of hocus-pocus. Everyone enjoys a little trickery, especially if no one is badly hurt. Plus, the story is plainly self-deprecating. It is the opposite of off-putting. Reagan isn't boasting. He isn't talking down to any-one. He's on our level and plainly at ease being there. This may be the narrative's most effective attribute, an example of what national political analysts would later describe as Reagan's aw-shucks style. He is mainly laughing at himself, as he highlights his imaginary foul-ball derby to cover what turns out to be a single-pitch infield pop-up out.

And notice something else: how it's all wrapped up in a know-ing wink. It's as if Reagan is saying without quite saying directly to the listener: *Yes, I totally invented that, but it's kinda funny, isn't it?* ... *And now you, too, are in on the joke.* That's a big part of what makes this kind of story so relatable: as listeners, we can imagine ourselves making the same decision under the same circumstances—and shaking our heads later at the ridiculousness of it all. Who hasn't been there? You know you need to do something. You aren't sure what. You have no time to think about it. You take the leap and hope for the best. What could be more human than that?

If there were a graduate school for storytelling, it could be the final exam.

Looking back at Reagan's time on the radio, we can see clear hints of so much more to come. Even back then, the future Great Communicator had a deeply developed sense of how to impart the most deeply relevant elements of the most deeply relevant issues. Not bad for a twenty-something. And it's striking how much his landmark speeches as president would be influenced by those early radio days. With coaching from station managers and other announcers, he learned to lose his Midwestern accent and develop a more sonorous style of speaking. He got comfortable improvising—something that would be extremely useful for press conferences, debates, and negotiations with America's enemies. He came to understand that, without strong characters, hardly anyone would pay attention to his stories. He practiced building his narratives around the contest and struggle between two opposing forces, one heroic, the other conniving. And if he had to fudge the facts a little . . . well, to a storytelling radio announcer, minor facts were just the raw material. And it all went back to those *heroic* Cubs.

I don't know if Reagan ever made a conscious connection between his sportscasting days and the powerful speeches he would deliver as president. He never said so directly, though the best of his speechwriters—Peggy Noonan and David Gergen at the top of the list—were true savants, picking up on that earlier style of his and the narrative preferences that went along with it.

It was no accident that Reagan would choose to single out worthy Americans each year at his State of the Union address. He began that tradition in 1982 when he invited a twenty-eight-year-old federal worker named Lenny Skutnik to be his special guest in the House gallery. Two weeks earlier, Air Florida Flight 90, Dulles to Tampa, had taken off in a snowstorm and crashed into the Potomac

River a mile from the Washington airport, killing seventy-eight people. During his address, Reagan pointed to Mr. Skutnik in the gallery and told the vast television audience: "In the midst of a terrible tragedy on the Potomac, we saw again the spirit of American heroism at its finest—the heroism of dedicated rescue workers saving crash victims from icy waters. And we saw the heroism of one of our young government employees, Lenny Skutnik, who, when he saw a woman lose her grip on the helicopter line, dived into the water and dragged her to safety."

Maybe the story resonated so strongly with the president because of his lifeguard days. But every year since, Reagan and all the other presidents have carried on that tradition, inviting heroic everyday Americans as guests for the State of the Union address. Still, all these years later, no one has mastered that storytelling flourish as movingly as Ronald Reagan.

That talent and instinct goes to a core Reagan belief: that the true greatness of America is rooted in the everyday heroism of our people. Inspiration comes not from the government or its leaders but from the acts of ordinary Americans raising their families, building their businesses, and supporting the causes they believe in. It was easy for Reagan to give voice to these ordinary Americans. He genuinely saw himself as one of them.

He liked to describe the world in terms of good and evil, *our* team and *their* team, *us* and *them*, never leaving any confusion about which side he was on. He always put the heroes first. If there was, say, a terrible, deadly fire, Reagan would start with the firefighters, then get to the victims. For Reagan, that hero could be an individual, a group of people, the Republican Party, or, writ even larger,

America. He certainly had no trouble casting others as villains. Liberal Democrats. Union loafers. Welfare queens. The Evil Empire. Those clear dividing lines were never in doubt with Reagan. They would define his public image through his governorship and his presidency. He liked to emphasize what was gained instead of what was lost. And the radio was where all of that first came alive.

In Reagan's hands, these stories usually had a larger point. He wasn't just telling idle tales. He had a political purpose or a national purpose or an ambition to change the culture somehow. He may not have publicly stated that purpose, but it was always top of mind. His stories were never told just for the stories' sake. They didn't hit you smack in the face. Instead, they brought you around gradually. They got you to the conclusion with fun, wonderful, quirky details. That was Reagan. He lured you in. Lenny Skutnik had the most boring job imaginable, anonymously toiling away in the Congressional Budget Office. On that awful day, he was sent home early because of the storm. But when he jumped into the icy river, he was transformed from an unassuming assistant into a national hero.

Reagan didn't use those stories just to entertain or inform the public. To him, they were also valuable tools for persuading his colleagues and his adversaries. It was an all-encompassing skill for him. Once Reagan started talking, he could disarm his critics without them even realizing he was trying to.

Look at the speech Reagan delivered on January 28, 1986, six hours after the space shuttle *Challenger* exploded during launch, killing all seven crew members aboard. Later in the book, we'll dive into the *Challenger* disaster in far greater detail. But I want to mention it here because that speech is such an exquisite example of

Reagan's unique storytelling style. He went right to the heroes and named them.

"Perhaps we've forgotten the courage it took for the crew of the shuttle," he said. "But they, the *Challenger* Seven, were aware of the dangers, but overcame them and did their jobs brilliantly. We mourn seven heroes: Michael Smith, Dick Scobee, Judith Resnik, Ronald McNair, Ellison Onizuka, Gregory Jarvis, and Christa McAuliffe. We mourn their loss as a nation together."

That afternoon, Reagan spoke directly to the families of the seven. "We cannot bear, as you do, the full impact of this tragedy. But we feel the loss, and we're thinking about you so very much. Your loved ones were daring and brave, and they had that special grace, that special spirit that says, 'Give me a challenge, and I'll meet it with joy.' They had a hunger to explore the universe and discover its truths. They wished to serve, and they did. They served all of us."

America that night was not a nation divided. It was a nation united by teary eyes.

I'll quote a lot more of it later, but I think we can all agree: that speech was a masterful performance by a former radio announcer who knew exactly how to strike the right chord.

CHAPTER 4

WALK OF FAME

In Hollywood, Reagan tasted success like he never had before. Money. Fame. A movie star wife . . . and, eventually, another. But just as his career was really taking off, America was pulled into war—and all bets were off.

LESSON LEARNED: NO MATTER HOW WELL THINGS ARE GOING, ALWAYS HAVE A BACKUP PLAN.

While Reagan was still on the radio in Des Moines, the Chicago Cubs held spring training on Santa Catalina Island, twenty-five miles off the coast of Los Angeles. This wasn't by accident. The late William Wrigley Jr., the chewing gum magnate who had been the Cubs' principal owner, had also owned the "Isle with a Smile," as he liked to call Catalina. He'd invested millions in the island's attractions and infrastructure, including a five-star hotel, the Catalina Casino, and a ballpark with a field whose dimensions precisely matched those of Chicago's Wrigley Field. Ringed by eucalyptus trees, the park was located below a mountaintop country club that housed the players' locker rooms and clubhouse. The patios provided a perfect left-field view of the action below, a West Coast version of the windows and rooftops along Wrigleyville's Waveland Avenue. The players certainly didn't complain. After long months of frigid temperatures in Chicagoland, the ocean vistas and Pacific breezes helped turn everyone's attention back to baseball.

In March of 1937, the twenty-six-year-old Reagan went out to cover the team. One night he was visiting in Los Angeles with Joy Hodges, a WHO Radio friend from Des Moines who was working in the movie business. The visiting sportscaster jokingly mentioned that he might like to "get into pictures." Joy had been around her former coworker long enough to notice he was a good-looking guy, six foot one, with wavy brown hair, blue eyes, and a warm, inviting baritone. She also remembered Dutch's stories about how much he enjoyed acting in high school and college.

She didn't ask permission. She just arranged a screen test for him. By the time Reagan left California and returned by train to Iowa, a six-month, $200-a-week contract with Warner Bros. was waiting in the mailbox for him. When he announced he'd be giving up his position at the radio station, an article in the *Des Moines Tribune* quoted him as saying in what was fast becoming his self-effacing style: "I may be out there for only the six months. Of course, I hope it doesn't turn out that way, but you never can tell."

And things moved at lightning speed from there.

He signed the deal with Warner Bros. on April 20. He cleared out his Des Moines apartment and headed west again by the end of May. On June 7, he reported to the studio for his first motion picture, a lighthearted drama called *Love Is on the Air.* There was, however, one issue Dutch Reagan hadn't counted on. The big bosses at Warner Bros. hated his name.

Who exactly was the freshest face in Hollywood supposed to be?

"So they called a meeting to discuss what my name should be," he recalled years later. "And I began to realize how expendable what you might call my identity was in this new business I was in."

Dutch was never an issue on the radio. No one had even questioned it. But apparently the name was a problem in the movies, though no one at the studio ever said exactly why, nor did they seem to care what the young actor might think. "As they were throwing names back and forth, I was just sitting there listening. They acted as if I couldn't hear." But they still hadn't come up with a new name.

"Finally," Reagan recalled, "as they kept going on and trying out various names, looking up as if they were looking at a marquee, I timidly suggested one they hadn't thought of, my real name. Ronald Reagan. They started tossing it around the table. And I'll never forget the scene. The top man said it over and over to himself: 'Ronald Reagan, Ronald Reagan.' He paused for a long moment and then declared, 'I like it.' So, I became Ronald Reagan."

And Ronald Reagan got right to work.

In *Love Is on the Air*, he plays Andy McCaine, a reckless radio reporter (what are the chances of that?) who gets into hot water for exposing people in high places. As punishment, his boss forces him to host a stupid kiddie program. While our hero advises his young listeners to eat their veggies and drink their milk, he also digs up enough dirt to nail the corrupt officials once and for all.

No one could confuse *Love Is on the Air* with fine cinema. But it was a likable picture and, for the handsome male lead, a thoroughly respectable Hollywood debut. He'd never been in a movie before, and immediately he was carrying one. And he was getting noticed . . . sometimes. The *New York Times* ignored the movie entirely, but the *Hollywood Reporter* wrote that Reagan was "a natural, giving one of the best first performances Hollywood has offered in many a day." The following year, 1938, he appeared in a fast succession of nine—count 'em, *nine*—back-to-back films in a wide variety of roles, some large, some tiny, all of them teaching the eager newcomer the business from the inside. Comedies. Dramas. Even musicals. Reagan wasn't a splendid singer, but he could definitely carry a tune. Warner Bros. was a busy studio with a roster of contract players who were cast over and over again. Though Reagan was still new in town, he was very much in the mix.

In *Sergeant Murphy*, he plays a cavalry private who trains an unloved horse to be a champion racer. In *Swing Your Lady*, a country musical–comedy with an outlandish wrestling theme, he has a totally forgettable role opposite Humphrey Bogart. In the drama *Accidents Will Happen*, Reagan stars again, as an insurance investigator who tangles with a crafty gang of fraudsters.

The producers and directors liked his comfort on camera and his get-it-done work ethic. *Read the script, learn the lines, shoot the scenes . . . and move on to the next one!* He was on his way to becoming a movie star, but he was still very much Nelle Reagan's diligent son.

Cowboy from Brooklyn is another musical romantic comedy,

this one starring Dick Powell, Pat O'Brien, and Priscilla Lane. *Girls on Probation* is meatier and darker. Reagan is a crusading attorney who defends an innocent party girl unfairly accused of stealing a dress. He is one of three leads in *Brother Rat*, which is set on the campus of Virginia Military Academy. This time Reagan's a good-natured troublemaker trying (and failing) to clean up his act before graduation. With him in *Brother Rat* is a busy studio player named Jane Wyman, a brown-eyed, button-nosed beauty best known for her sentimental, "four-hankie" roles. Over the next two years, they would appear together in three more films (the sequel *Brother Rat and a Baby*, *An Angel from Texas*, and *Tugboat Annie Sails Again*). Everyone agreed the pair had excellent chemistry. When they started dating, the commute couldn't have been any easier. They both had apartments in Londonderry in West Hollywood.

Wyman's upbringing made Reagan's look almost affluent and secure. Her parents divorced when she was three. Her father died when she was four. Her mother turned her over to the Missouri foster care system. At age eleven she moved to Southern California with her foster mother, bouncing between there and St. Joseph, Missouri, where her foster father still lived and was chief of detectives. After dropping out of high school at fifteen, Jane lied about her age, moved back to Hollywood, and began her acting career, signing a deal with Warner Bros. a year before Reagan did. And unlike Reagan she'd been married before. To Nelle, she seemed a little . . . *fast*. "I was in hopes he would fall in love with some sweet girl who is not in the movies," Nelle confided to friends.

Oh, well.

They married on January 26, 1940, at the Irish-themed Wee Kirk o' the Heather chapel on the grounds of the vast Forest Lawn Memorial Park in Glendale. It was a simple ceremony amid a sea of tombstones. But the movie magazines and the gossip columns loved every second of it, almost as much as the Warner Bros. PR people did.

The newlyweds moved into his apartment and Jane gave up hers while they completed construction on a new house on Cordell Drive in Beverly Hills and both of them pressed full speed ahead with their busy acting careers. Along the way, Reagan appeared in four films as Secret Service agent Brass Bancroft, including *Murder in the Air*, and grabbed one of the most memorable roles of his career, as Notre Dame football player George Gipp in *Knute Rockne All American*. Out of that one, Reagan got a new nickname, "the Gipper," and a line of dialogue that would later translate seamlessly into politics: "Win one for the Gipper."

Life was sweet in Hollywood, which felt like at least a million miles from Iowa and Illinois.

The acting role he was proudest of was playing a double amputee in 1942's *Kings Row*, which was nominated for Best Picture at the 15th Academy Awards. In that film, he gets to yank on the heartstrings with the memorable line "Where's the rest of me?" Reagan liked the line so much, he would use it as the title of his first autobiography, in 1965. Though the *New York Times* panned the movie as "gloomy and ponderous," the film soared at the box office, and it was the role Reagan believed "made me a star."

Unfortunately, his timing was terrible. He wasn't able to capitalize on that success anywhere near as much as he hoped to. One day after *Kings Row* hit theaters, four months after Japanese warplanes bombed Pearl Harbor, with World War II already raging, Ronald Reagan was called up to active duty in the U.S. Army. He would never recapture the full measure of Hollywood glory he had worked so hard to achieve over the previous five years.

Reagan didn't feel "a burning desire to be an army officer," as he would readily concede years later. He was too young for World War I, seven when that conflict ended. He went straight from high school to college and straight to work from there—as *straight* as the Depression allowed for. But just before he left Iowa for Hollywood, he'd signed up for the Army Enlisted Reserves—mainly, it seems, because he'd always wanted to ride a horse. The 322nd Cavalry Regiment conducted equestrian training at Fort Des Moines, and Reagan was promptly promoted to second lieutenant. When he arrived in Los Angeles, he transferred his reserve duty to the 323rd Cavalry, which taught horsemanship to civilians through the citizens' military training camp at the Presidio of Monterey, two hours south of San Francisco.

Being in the reserves wasn't much of a time commitment: occasional weekends up the coast and an annual summer camp. And Reagan got hours in the saddle, a nice thing to mention on his acting résumé. None of this interfered with his busy production schedule . . . until suddenly *it did*.

Lieutenant Reagan was ordered to active duty on April 19, 1942. The horses were sent out to pasture. The 323rd was converted into a tank destroyer battalion. Due to his poor eyesight, Reagan was classified "limited service only," which kept him from deploying overseas with the tank battalion. When he arrived for his physical at Fort Mason in the northern Marina District of San Francisco, the doctor warned him, "If we sent you overseas, you'd shoot a general."

"And you'd miss him," one of the doctor's colleagues quickly added.

Since Reagan had been in the reserves for more than five years, the men conducting the physical wondered how he'd gotten past his previous eye exam.

"Well," Reagan admitted in that genial way of his, "I cheated."

When he struck that tone, it was almost impossible to argue with him.

Clearly, the actor-soldier did not anticipate a long career in uniform. He was invited for dinner with a superior officer, Colonel Phillip Booker. Natural bonder that he was, Reagan remarked to the colonel that they had something in common.

"How's that, Reagan?" the colonel asked gruffly. The other dinner guests, all with higher ranks, leaned in to hear the answer.

With confidence he would later attribute to being a trained actor and having just consumed two pre-dinner martinis, Reagan answered: "Well, I understand you are a graduate of Virginia Military Institute. I once played in a picture about V.M.I. called *Brother Rat.*"

The colonel sat up even straighter than he had been sitting. "Yes, Reagan," he said. "I saw that picture—nothing ever made me so damn mad." But Reagan reached back to the empathy he'd learned as a boy and the natural, human connectivity he'd been honing forever. Somehow, a smile and shrug from him was all it took. In another few seconds, the colonel's unpleasant manner was gone.

Ronald and Jane were settled into their new house by then. Their first child, daughter Maureen, had celebrated her first birthday in January. And the studio made sure that photographers got pictures of the three of them saying goodbye as Reagan left for his first active-duty assignment as a liaison officer at the San Francisco Port of Embarkation. But the family wasn't apart for long. On June 9, at the urging of Warner Bros., Lieutenant Reagan was transferred to the Army Air Forces public relations staff and the First Motion Picture Unit in Culver City, which Jack Warner had helped establish.

Known as FMPU and pronounced "fum-poo," the unit produced Frank Capra's "Why We Fight" series as well as a documentary about the *Memphis Belle*, a Boeing B-17 Flying Fortress whose crew completed twenty-five missions against enemy targets in Europe. Six months later, Reagan was promoted to *first* lieutenant and dispatched to the Provisional Task Force unit producing *This Is the Army* in Burbank, a nine-minute drive from the Warner Bros. lot, a bit more during rush hour.

Every military assignment has its challenges, of course. But, no, these weren't quite the equivalent of storming the beaches at Normandy.

Lieutenant (and just six months later Captain) Reagan served his country as a personnel officer, a post adjutant, an executive officer, an actor, and a narrator. He spent nine months in New York City opening a War Loan Drive. By the time his active duty ended on September 10, 1945, more than three years after he reported to Fort Mason, his units had produced nearly four hundred training, morale, and propaganda films, including *Rear Gunner*, *Jap Zero*, *For God and Country*, and *Beyond the Line of Duty*. And millions of Americans got to see the patriotic actor in a new screen role as the cinematic face of the U.S. military, whose deployment he vigorously supported from the vital trenches of Hollywood.

What a rude surprise was waiting for him!

As he returned to civilian life, Ronald Reagan felt like he had done what his country had asked him to. Though he never saw combat overseas, a great war effort requires many hands engaged in many different activities, and Reagan knew he had performed every task he'd been assigned. Now, like millions of other American servicemen after V-E and V-J Day, he was ready to pick up his life where he'd left it and resume his chosen career. But was Hollywood ready for his triumphant return?

Not so much, it seemed.

In the three years Reagan had been out of the business, something had changed for him. He wasn't one of the golden boys at Warner Bros. anymore, plopped into every project that came along. At thirty-four, he certainly wasn't the hot new thing. It had been a long time since those bright blue eyes had stared down from a color movie poster or *Starring Ronald Reagan* was illuminated on a theater marquee. Tastes change. Audiences move on. Had Reagan lost his sizzle? That's what the studio executives seemed to believe. He couldn't help but feel a difference in the kinds of roles he was being considered for now.

Where was the next *Kings Row?* Where was the next *Knute Rockne All American?* They were going to some new, younger leading man. Reagan always believed World War II cost him his chance to reach the top in Hollywood. By the end of the war, his big-screen moment had clearly passed, never to return again.

As you might have heard—and Reagan certainly had: Hollywood can be cruel.

It wasn't that the studio execs wouldn't cast him in *anything.* It was the *kinds* of pictures they now thought he was suitable for, movies that he considered two or three rungs beneath him. *The Voice of the Turtle. John Loves Mary. The Girl from Jones Beach.* Really . . . ? Reagan wanted to work. He took the roles. But it wouldn't be too much longer before he was co-starring with a trained chimpanzee in *Bedtime for Bonzo.*

Later on, when his political enemies wanted to diminish him or make his time in the movie business sound inconsequential, these postwar movies were always the ones they'd point to. In fact, Reagan wouldn't entirely disagree. He craved meaty roles he could really sink his teeth into. Instead, he kept being planted in B-movie thrillers and cast as the genial doofus in lightweight comedies, where he never got to do much on the screen.

He grew quickly disgusted.

He tried to reverse his altered fortunes. He kept reminding people in the industry that he was prepared to do a whole lot more. But he could also see that it was probably a losing cause. Around that time, he was also dealing with issues at home. He and Jane Wyman had two children now, after adopting son Michael. But the old chemistry had clearly faded. They had a baby, Christine, who was born prematurely and died the next day, a trauma for any couple. They weren't fighting openly, but after nine years of marriage, a certain chilly distance had set in. The made-in-Hollywood duo whose smiling faces once had people going "Awwww . . ." were now on the road to divorce. She filed in the summer of 1948. They were on and off two or three times, and he seemed to hold out hope until the very end. One Hollywood tabloid quoted him as saying, "It's a strange character I'm married to. But—I love her." The reporter noted Reagan spoke those words with a tender smile. Still, in July of 1949, they called it quits for good.

A registered Republican, Wyman blamed the breakup on political differences with her avid Democrat of a husband. No doubt, but there was also more to it than that. It was hard not to notice that, while Reagan was making routine training films for the Army, her career was positively soaring. She'd won raves for her wrenching portrayal of an alcoholic's fiancée in *The Lost Weekend*. She snagged an Academy Award nomination for *The Yearling*. She'd go on to win a best-actress Oscar for *Johnny Belinda*, in which she played a deaf teenager who was raped. All while Reagan's Hollywood career was undeniably on the downslide. There were no more agents itching to sign him, no more producers eager to cast him, no more showbiz writers clamoring for a five-minute interview. His happy dash to stardom was clearly running out of gas. And he certainly wasn't getting any younger, not in movie star years.

He knew he needed to do something . . . but *what*?

It wasn't like Reagan to feel sorry for himself. Despite his altered circumstances, he still had his cheerful disposition and abiding optimism. And he had plenty of energy. He hadn't lost that. As the pressure built around him, he managed to channel Nelle again, the mother who'd been such a role model for resilience, no matter what the odds might be. She never folded under pressure far greater than what he was now experiencing. Though he was being tested, he wouldn't fold, either. He'd find some other way to succeed. Fifteen years out of Illinois and Iowa, he was still his mother's son. As he came to grips with the new reality of his situation, he went looking for something important to do. Something important to other people. Something important to himself.

He found it at his local union hall.

Back in the day, it used to be that actors were paid once for being in a movie. No matter how many tickets were sold. No matter how many times the movie ran on television. No matter how long the side-stream profits kept pouring in for the studios and their executives. It was one and done for those whose faces graced the screen.

When the union known as the Screen Actors Guild was being organized in the years before World War II, many actors felt badly exploited by the big studios. They wanted better wages and saner hours. They wanted health insurance and a retirement plan. But the main thing they wanted, especially in the postwar years as television became a bigger factor, was residuals, the chance to share in the revenues when their work was suddenly appearing in people's living rooms.

Weren't they the ones the audiences were tuning in for? It wasn't the ugly mugs of Jack Warner, Louis Mayer, Adolph Zukor, or Darryl Zanuck . . . was it? But the studio bosses had an answer when the actors' union demanded a piece of the extra action.

"Over our dead bodies!" Warner, Mayer, Zukor, Zanuck, and their Hollywood brethren roared, nearly in unison. They worried, and for good reason, that if they started sharing the back end with the actors, it wouldn't be long before the directors, the screenwriters, and probably the theater snack-bar attendants all had their hands out too.

Ronald Reagan had been a guild member since he first arrived in town. He paid his $25 initiation fee and became a "union man," though not an especially active one. Not at first. He joined the SAG board in 1941 as the rep for new actors. But it wasn't until after the war, when he felt his own career flagging, that he really threw himself into the union cause. On March 10, 1947, when actor Robert Montgomery resigned mid-term as guild president, Reagan was tapped to replace him.

He didn't campaign for the position. He wasn't even in the board meeting when the first vote was taken. But he was flattered by the confidence of his fellow actors, and he was thrilled to have something new to focus on. Better than getting depressed about roles he didn't get! As he'd learned from Nelle, when one door is closing, you have to yank on another one—*hard*. And he threw himself into the union role, working to improve the wages, pensions, and working conditions of his fellow actors. The studio executives didn't like negotiating any more than they ever had, and they certainly didn't give in to Reagan's every demand. But they generally found him to be a genial and respectful adversary, a union leader who wouldn't abandon his or his members' principles but was always open to reasonable compromise—and always pleasant about it.

Reagan had clearly learned the lesson of disagreeing without being disagreeable, a balance that would serve him greatly for the rest of his life.

In those days Hollywood was a hotbed of political intrigue, and Reagan couldn't help being drawn into some of it. It wasn't just the usual debates between New Deal liberals and small-government conservatives. As the Cold War heated up, the FBI was investigating claims that Communists had infiltrated the industry, hoping to spread their message to America through movies and TV. Various smaller unions were tied to the reds. Was the actors' union too? Prodded by Wisconsin senator Joe McCarthy, Congress was eager to find out. Some of the studios had drawn up "blacklists" of writers, directors, and actors who were thought to have ties to the Communists, vowing not to hire them.

The House Un-American Activities Committee was taking a hard look at Hollywood. The committee members were eager for an insider to speak with and ultimately landed on Ronald Reagan. When he was called to testify on October 23, 1947, he'd been SAG president for barely seven months, but he couldn't exactly duck the issue. He didn't name names when he sat before the committee, though he conceded that "a small clique" of SAG members "has been suspected of more or less following the tactics that we associated with the Communist Party."

"What steps should be taken to rid the motion picture industry of any Communist influences?" he was asked.

In his answer, Reagan walked a dicey line, standing up for the majority of his members while mostly downplaying the threat. What he wanted most of all, it seemed, was to keep the guild out of the line of fire. "Well, sir," he said, "ninety-nine percent of us are pretty well aware of what is going on.... I think within the bounds of our democratic rights and never once stepping over the rights given us by democracy, we have done a pretty good job in our business of keeping those people's activities curtailed.... I can certainly testify that in the case of the Screen Actors Guild, we have been eminently successful in preventing them from, with their usual tactics, trying to run a majority of an organization with a well-organized minority."

His main strategy, it seemed, was to talk without saying too much, a skill more associated with Washington than Hollywood. He quoted the Founding Fathers and emphasized the people's right to dissent. "I believe that, as Thomas Jefferson put it, if all the American people know all of the facts, they will never make a mistake." In the end, Reagan got safely in and out of Washington, a deft performance at a difficult time. His testimony to Congress also got him a flurry of attention in the media, where several commentators expressed surprise that he seemed to speak with such passion about politics. Maybe he was more than another lightweight actor or another knee-jerk union boss, they allowed. Whatever the expectations, Reagan beat them. And when all the tussling over Communists in Hollywood finally settled down, he was able to focus again on wages, pensions, working conditions, and the heaviest lift of all: film-to-TV residuals.

It was Reagan proving once again that effective leadership

needs to be persuasive, persistent, and willing at times to accept incremental victories while also ducking the unexpected threats when they arrive. He really came to understand this in Hollywood.

One important coda to Reagan's union service and the dicey times: on November 15, 1949, during his second year as SAG president, he had a meeting with an MGM contract player named Nancy Davis, who had discovered that her name was included on one of the McCarthy-era Hollywood blacklists. Unfairly, the guild actress said. She was clearly upset. She didn't know where to turn. She asked for Reagan's help maintaining her employment in the film industry and getting her name removed from the list.

Reagan agreed to look into it.

When he called back, he informed her that she had been confused with another Nancy Davis. He promised to clear up any lingering misunderstandings and be sure she maintained her right to keep working in her chosen field.

She thanked the union president and said she appreciated his help very much. They promised to stay in touch.

CHAPTER 5

COMPANY MAN

Just when he needed it most, Reagan was handed an unexpected opportunity. It not only changed his fortunes and his sagging Hollywood career. It also changed his mind.

LESSON LEARNED: YOU NEVER KNOW WHERE THE NEXT POSSIBILITY WILL LEAD.

There is nothing quite like being yesterday's news in Hollywood.

You're still famous. You still have the houses and the cars and the tan you acquired when you were the toast of the town. The agents and studio executives still know who you are, even if they don't return your calls as quickly as they used to. But for a fading actor, even a former star, the wide smiles and warm handshakes are like so much else in Hollywood: they quickly point in other directions when a has-been says hello.

So it was for Ronald Reagan in 1954.

His five-year run as guild president was over. He figured he'd done what he could and was ready to move on. He was married by then to Nancy Davis, the actress he'd freed from the blacklist, and starting to feel financially squeezed. The house in Pacific Palisades needed furniture. He was also paying bills on a weekend place, a 305-acre ranch in the hills of Malibu, where land values were soaring but so were the property taxes. He was writing child-support checks to Jane and covering private-school tuitions for Maureen and Michael. Daughter Patti, his first child with Nancy, was two years old. And the roles he'd been getting? If anything, they'd gotten even worse. He was the English professor who tried to save "Hot Garters Gertie," a burlesque dancer turned college coed, in the musical comedy *She's Working Her Way Through College*. At least his co-star that time was *human*. In *Bedtime for Bonzo*, where he had been paired with the rambunctious chimpanzee, people were still debating whether he or the ape was the co-star. Where was the next *Knute Rockne All American*, the next *Kings Row*, the next *good* role? Obviously, they were going to some new heartthrob.

Was this all there was?

To make ends meet, Reagan did something that hadn't been part of the equation since his radio days: commercials. He appeared in ads for Van Heusen dress shirts and a men's hair grooming product called Wildroot Cream Oil, "infused with lanolin!" He turned to old pals and snagged occasional guest spots on the Milton Berle and Burns and Allen variety shows as network radio slowly migrated to network TV. The low point might have been climbing into a straw hat and bow tie to emcee a Las Vegas lounge act at the aptly named Hotel Last Frontier. Reagan brought on a dancing acrobatic troupe, a barbershop quartet, and the Blackburn Twins, featuring

Evelyn Ward, a Broadway showgirl who happened to be the mother of future pop star David Cassidy. The house chorus line was nicknamed the Adorabelles. Reagan was an amiable emcee, hamming it up for laughs and joining some of the zany sketches. He belted out a serviceable "Sweet Adeline." And most nights the house was full. But after the two-week run, there was no return engagement. This certainly wasn't where he expected to be at forty-three years old.

Then one day Reagan's luck changed.

His agents at MCA had set up a company to produce a weekly TV show called *General Electric Theater*. Would he like to host?

Reagan was skeptical at first. As a successful film star, did he really want to hitch his wagon to a television show hawking toasters and light bulbs? Though TV was clearly on the rise, "Everyone of stature in Hollywood was delicately holding their noses about it," he recalled later. "My personal interest in television was nil." Then he heard that Cary Grant, William Holden, and even Jane Wyman had already appeared on the program and that Jack Benny and Bob Hope were penciled in for the new season, and suddenly whatever lingering doubts he had were swept away. Who was he kidding? It had to beat Vegas in a straw hat.

For Reagan in 1954, *General Electric Theater* wasn't just a piece of steady work in a business not known for steadiness. It wasn't just a corporate-sweetened lifeline for an actor whose prospects didn't live up to his past. This was big, bigger by far than he even realized when he sent back word, "I'm in." This job would do more than rescue a needy actor. It would become Ronald Reagan's ticket to a whole new Ronald Reagan.

Thank God for lucky breaks—and grabbing the opportunities that presented themselves. Just keep moving forward. Forward . . . always.

The show aired Sunday nights at 9:00 eastern and Pacific time on CBS. It had a unique, fairly highbrow premise: each episode adapted a novel, short story, play, or film. Sometimes a comedy, sometimes a drama. With rotating directors and rotating casts. For Reagan, it was an easy gig, and it paid $125,000 a season plus a generous expense account—real money in 1954, even in Hollywood. His job was to be likable as he introduced the scenes, provide some much-needed continuity, and cast GE in a flattering light, so to speak. When Reagan debuted as host on September 26, 1954, the show had already been running for a year and a half. As the GE execs quickly discovered, this guy Reagan had exactly what the show needed, whatever that was. They were sure of this much: the fading movie star had the familiarity and comfort to carry thirty minutes of network television. The Nielsen ratings shot up immediately, from a number 27 ranking in 1953–54 to number 3 in 1955–56, reaching more than 25 million viewers a week. Only *I Love Lucy* and *The Ed Sullivan Show* grabbed more eyeballs. And Reagan wasn't only welcoming the audience and introducing the sketches. He was also appearing in some of them. And the moment could hardly be any more propitious. This was just as television was coming into its own—and discovering what a powerful force it could be. Reagan might not be in the glamorous movie house releases anymore. But all of a sudden he was somewhere even better. He was in everyone's living room, a literal household name. Since his deal with GE included a piece of the action, the has-been actor and ex–union chief was suddenly raking in bigger money than he'd ever made before.

Over time, the TV audience got to meet his photogenic family, especially his actress wife, Nancy. Several broadcasts brought viewers into the Reagans' "all-electric hilltop home" in Pacific Palisades, which GE outfitted with all the latest better-living gizmos. See the retractable roof over the atrium. Check out the automatic skillet, the steam-and-dry iron, and the underwater lights in the heated pool. All the family's "electrical servants . . . make Mommy's work easier," Nancy confides in one segment to three-year-old Patti. "That's why every housewife wants them, the latest models with the newest improvements."

Thank you, GE!

None of this was a stretch for Reagan, who genuinely believed in the power of science and technology to help everyone lead richer, better, safer, more comfortable lives. Hadn't medical researchers just found a vaccine for polio? Hadn't powerful weapons helped win World War II?

GE couldn't get enough of Reagan . . . or the Reagans. And neither could the audience.

At the same time he was hosting the TV show, Reagan was made a "traveling ambassador" for the company, heading out across the country to speak to the employees and tout the wonders of living better electrically. GE wasn't only huge. It was hugely spread out. The company made everything from washers and dryers to power plant turbines to airplane parts. One by one, Reagan visited all of GE's 139 factories, labs, and other facilities and ended up addressing well over half of the company's 250,000 employees. He hated flying, so he took the train and sometimes made as many as a dozen speeches a day. Grip-and-grins with the shirt-and-tie men in the offices. Rah-rah sessions with the sales teams. Lunches in the workers' cafeteria. Tours of the factory floors. He also did loads of local appearances in the places he visited, community events at social organizations, sit-downs with city and town notables, talking up General Electric and listening to his hosts explain whatever the local issues might be. At night he'd swing by a Rotary or Kiwanis meeting before heading back to the motel. This turned out to be an amazing educational opportunity, a chance to interact one-on-one with quite a cross-section of GE employees and their neighbors. He listened to their hopes and apprehensions. He learned about their jobs and families. He BS'ed in the break rooms and at the water coolers. He became as good a listener as he was a talker, something very few public communicators are able to say.

Many of the people he met were regular working-class Americans. Lots of them felt squeezed financially, as he recently had, and nobody liked paying taxes! Up close and in person, he was seeing who Americans really were, what they hoped for, what they worried about, what they wanted, and what they didn't—knowledge that would help tailor his messages for decades to come. Reagan had one of the underrated traits of great leadership. An attentive, empathetic listener, he would maintain that powerful skill throughout his career.

"I was seeing the same people that I grew up with in Dixon,

Illinois," he recalled. "I realized I was living in a tinsel factory. And this exposure brought me back."

Could there be a better AAA ball for major-league politics?

It was on those packed speaking tours that Reagan learned how to work a live audience, how to boil complex ideas into digestible nuggets, how to deliver just the right degree of self-deprecation, which jokes landed and which ones flopped. Through sheer repetition and trial and error, he became an expert at coming across as a warm, relatable personality instead of a nose-in-the-air movie star. And he learned to love it. If only more politicians could spend such extended time in person, patiently listening, instead of pretending to listen while campaigning, one eye on the person's face, the other on the exit—with a hand reaching for the voter's wallet!

At every one of those stops, Reagan would share the company's vision of the world, which was bullish on American ingenuity and bearish on government regulators sticking their nose in everything. Though he helped select the topics he spoke about and crafted a lot of the language, the materials came from General Electric headquarters in Schenectady, New York. Of course, the company took a dim view of corporate taxation, government intrusion, foreign competition, and labor unions.

He'd open his talks on a jokey note, the movie star from California showing the locals he, too, was a regular guy. But he'd segue quickly into the meat of the matter, making his political points in everyday terms. "Thirty-four percent of your phone bill is taxed, and twenty-seven percent of gas and oil use, and more than a fourth of the automobile you drive is in direct and indirect taxes," he would say. He'd bemoan the out-of-sight medical bills that his family also paid and warn against the evils of socialized medicine.

"Freedom," earnestly add, "is never more than one generation from extinction."

General Electric at that time was well known for its anti-union stance, and that could have been an issue for Reagan. But the former SAG president didn't seem to flinch at this sort of outreach. He'd had his own issues with the unions in Los Angeles, some of which he really did believe were under communist sway. He seemed to have no problem helping to persuade GE employees that the company really did care about them. After all, hadn't they taken good care of *him*? His stated and unstated message to the GE workforce: Strikes don't solve anything, no matter how legitimate the workers' frustrations are. Always better to work things out with a company that truly cares about its employees—a company like GE.

This time for Reagan, as he put it later, was a "postgraduate course in political science" and an "apprenticeship for public life." You could also call it a practice run for a political career . . . from the other side of the street than the one he'd previously lived on.

Raised in a New Deal family, steeped in liberal Hollywood, leading a major trade union, it would have been surprising if Reagan *hadn't* arrived at GE with some strong liberal instincts. In fact, his journey to the right wasn't quite as straight a line as people like to remember, just as Hollywood in those Cold War years wasn't quite the leftie cliché that hindsight makes it out to be. If anything, Reagan was near the front of that curve. Though he voted for Democrat Harry Truman in the 1948 presidential election, he backed Republican Dwight Eisenhower in 1952 and 1956, finding Democrat Adlai Stevenson too soft on communism. Reagan had plenty of conservative Hollywood friends in those postwar years, even in the SAG leadership: right-leaning actors like Dick Powell, Robert Taylor, George Murphy, and Robert Montgomery, who preceded Reagan as union president. As far as those guys were concerned, it wasn't just Communists who posed a threat. Liberals were suspect, too, a constant menace to the industry and to the country. "Something should be done about it!" they were often quick to add. And those weren't the only conservative voices in Reagan's head.

His older brother, Neil, who'd followed him to Hollywood and worked as a television producer and advertising man, was a staunch conservative. So were Nancy's parents, especially her stepfather, Dr. Loyal Edward Davis, a prominent neurosurgeon who'd moved the family to Chicago. And in those years, Reagan had his own frustrating battles with the IRS, which couldn't have elevated the esteem he felt for large, intrusive government bureaucracies. He'd worked hard, become successful, and the thanks he'd gotten was the heavy hand of his government reaching deeper and deeper into his bank account. He was in the 87-percent tax bracket, something he never forgot.

All that said, as he settled into the GE orbit, he was, at the very least, open to a diversity of ideas. And those ideas didn't come only from the plant floor employees or the townsfolk he met. On those long train rides, as he worked on his speeches and watched the country go by, he had plenty of time to think. He also had Lemuel Boulware back at GE headquarters and Earl Dunckel in the train seat beside him.

Boulware was GE's vice president for labor relations, known for his take-it-or-leave-it approach to union negotiations. Boulware had made a name for himself as a tough negotiator during a 1946 general strike by the United Electrical, Radio and Machine Workers of America, and he considered pro-union Democrats his (and the country's) mortal enemies.

Dunckel was the GE public relations man assigned to Reagan's speaking tours. An ex–newspaper reporter from Schenectady and a proud conservative, Dunckel had a more conversational approach. He liked to quote F. A. Hayek, Whittaker Chambers, Ayn Rand, and other brainy icons of the right. He devoured *National Review*, which William F. Buckley had launched in 1954, giving American conservatism an intellectual home. Dunckel loved a friendly but rousing debate, as did Reagan. The two men passed their hours mixing it up over Harry Truman, FDR, the New Deal, communism, unions, war, peace, and taxes, with the company PR man slowly making progress with his conservative case.

"I was drumbeating this at him all the time," Dunckel told an interviewer nearly three decades later. "Whenever he tried to defend New Dealism, or what was passing for it at the time, we would have some rather spirited arguments. I think this helped him to realize, as he put it later, that he didn't desert the Democratic Party, that the Democratic Party deserted him."

There was a moment, as Dunckel recalled, when Reagan decided that "the gap had widened just too far to be bridged, that he was, he thought, following along the same path he'd always been on, but that the Democratic Party had veered off and left him. He found himself in so many things marching parallel with the Republicans."

With Boulware and Dunckel lodged in his head, Reagan's GE speeches reflected an increasingly political tone, going far beyond the wonders of electric kitchen appliances and general conservative themes to all the hot-button issues of the day. He denounced Social Security, federal aid to education, public housing, federal farm programs, and public utilities as threats to freedom and the American way. He lit into excessive government regulation, idiotic bureaucratic rules, clumsy attempts at social engineering, and welfare-loving Democrats. He warned his audiences about "the swiftly rising tide of collectivism that threatens to inundate what remains of our free economy." He took special aim at the electrical workers' union, which he said was "suffering from Communist infiltration amounting to outright domination" and spoke of an "attempted take-over of the industry by the Communists."

The writer Jacob Weisberg, who has carefully explored this phase of Reagan's life, is convinced that this is where the future president's pivot really occurred, though the change was also an outgrowth of Reagan's earliest years. "Here, to pin it down, is Reagan's decisive break with New Deal liberalism, and the first developed expression of his philosophical alternative," Weisberg writes in *Ronald Reagan*, part of the American Presidents Series. As a product of the American upper class, Weisberg notes, Roosevelt considered unregulated capitalism a dire threat to the people, and government regulation their best protector. By contrast, "Reagan, coming from the American lower middle class, now saw those roles reversed: taxation and regulation were the villains, corporations and markets his heroes." Years before Lyndon Johnson's Great Society and the Civil Rights Act, Reagan was already calling the continued expansion of federal authority not just wasteful, but the primary threat to individual liberty.

For Reagan, the path was set.

It took another six years for him to switch his party registration. But he wasn't quoting FDR so much anymore. Should he continue in this political vein, his own future clearly lay with the Republicans. In 1959, speaking to a packed ballroom of GE executives at New York's Waldorf-Astoria hotel, Reagan warned in dire terms about the perils of government expansion. It used to be, Reagan said, that the post office was the main contact Americans had with the federal government. "Today," he asserted, "there is hardly a phase of our daily living that doesn't feel the stultifying hand of government regulation and interference." Government bureaucracies, he added, had become "the very essence of totalitarianism."

Reagan saw the increasing use of the levers of government power as anti-conservative. What would he think today when Democrats use executive power to eliminate student debt without the assent of Congress? Or when Republicans use executive power to sue companies that disagree with the actions of the executive branch of government? I know what he would think. He would shake his head with disgust and amazement.

That November, while Reagan was still hosting *General Electric Theater* and traveling America for GE, the board of the Screen Actors Guild lured him back to serve another one-year term as president, just long enough to wrap up a piece of unfinished business from his previous five-year run. This time he finally got the residual payments that actors had long been dreaming of. It was quite a juxtaposition, the spokesman for the strongly anti-union General Electric company also leading one of Hollywood's most prominent unions. But there you have it: the board had faith in Reagan's political skills. He believed his fellow actors deserved to get paid when their films aired on TV. And he pulled it off, winning pension benefits for pre-1959 theatrical films and cash residuals for films made after that—payments that continue until today. It turned out the high-profile GE spokesman could also be a highly effective union leader. In an increasingly divided nation, that was really saying something.

So, how did he do it?

Well, a lot of it was Reagan's personal charm and his understanding of one-on-one human dynamics. After spending all those years wandering the America that wasn't Los Angeles or New York, he could make the case in a way that struck a lot of people as downright sensible. Just as important, he always expressed a willingness to compromise. He didn't need to *destroy* his adversaries. He just wanted to *reason* with them. What he hadn't been able to pull off before—what no one had—he finally managed to achieve.

While Reagan's outspokenness brought a smile to Boulware and Dunckel, it wasn't universally appreciated in the GE boardroom or the C-suite. There would come a time when Reagan's journey to the right would go too far for the comfort of some GE executives, who worried that their national spokesman's political views might be turning off some potential customers. Democrats buy vacuum cleaners, too, the bosses pointed out. Some even ran the organizations that order jet engines and high-tech medical devices.

Reagan was still in hot demand. "By the early 1960s," he wrote in *An American Life*, "GE was receiving more speaking invitations for me from around the country than I could handle." But somehow, his label had changed. Though he was delivering the same smaller-government message he'd delivered during the Eisenhower years, he wrote, he was suddenly being called a right-wing extremist. "The liberals just didn't like to hear someone say the growth of government ought to be restrained." With John Kennedy in the White House by then and a big piece of GE's business tied to defense contracts, Reagan could hang on only so long. In March of 1962, the company pulled the plug on the Sunday-night TV show, which had been losing ratings to NBC's *Bonanza*, and also dropped Reagan as a traveling ambassador, finally ending his plant visits and speaking tours.

He didn't like being fired, of course. Who does? But, upon reflection, he could see what almost everyone else could: he'd had a fabulous eight-year run that had increased his fame, broadened his appeal, supercharged his finances, rescued his career, taught him new performance skills, and given him a whole new way of looking at the world. Oh, and filled his California home with some pretty snazzy upgrades. Some of the sting was eased when his brother, Neil, landed him a contract to host *Death Valley Days*, a popular Western series sponsored by the company that made the laundry product 20 Mule Team Borax.

It wasn't just that a "great communicator" was nurtured in those eight years with General Electric. By the time he parted ways with the company, Ronald Reagan had not only enhanced his skills in front of an audience. He'd also learned exactly what he wanted to communicate, a kind of conservatism that was grounded in the soil of fifty-state America, a principled conservatism based on common sense and even some compromise, a message he already knew would connect with regular folks.

Clearly, there were no hard feelings on GE's side. "In token of our appreciation for your personal interest," General Electric vice president J. Stanford Smith wrote to Reagan in a gracious thank-you note, "we would like to replace the appliances you now have in your home with our newest models."

CHAPTER 6

HIS WAY

With The Speech, Reagan revealed to America—and to himself—what he really believed in . . . and where he was prepared to compromise. These were the formulations that would carry him into the governor's office and beyond.

LESSON LEARNED: DECLARE WHAT YOU REALLY BELIEVE IN, BUT STILL BE OPEN TO COMPROMISE.

Nineteen sixty-four was the year Ronald Reagan found his footing on the national political stage. And a speech is what helped him do it.

Though the General Electric company had moved on from its increasingly opinionated spokesman, millions of Americans were just getting to know that side of Reagan. He'd already been a sportscaster, a movie star, a union leader, and a popular CBS television host. What he had going for him at this phase of his career were all the lessons he had learned from the earlier ones—and a clarity of vision he had earned the hard way: on factory tours, at local-business luncheons, and on those long, long train rides with Earl Dunckel.

Now he had a much clearer view of what he thought the nation needed. He also had a clearer view of himself.

On the radio, he had learned to express himself with the deftness of a professional broadcaster. In Hollywood, he had learned how to project a low-key public image that audiences would naturally flock to. As president of the Screen Actors Guild, he had learned to advocate for others and on behalf of a cause. At GE, he'd shifted right and finally sorted out what he really believed in. Less government. More freedom. The traditional values that America was founded on: hard work, free enterprise, family, faith, self-sufficiency, and just enough compassion when people needed it but not so much as to create lifelong dependency. Reagan had no day job and no regular paycheck anymore, though with four children, two houses, a wife, and an ex-wife, he had a pricey lifestyle and a big monthly nut. But, thankfully, he also had a powerful tool at his command.

He had The Speech, and it was golden.

The capital *T* is intentional. It wasn't *a* speech. It was *The* Speech, a carefully crafted, well-practiced compendium of the things Reagan felt passionate about at that point in his life. He'd been working on The Speech for years. It was never *exactly* the same two nights in a row. He tweaked the language, adjusted the flow, inserted local references, and hammered different themes in front of different audiences. But the bones of The Speech were always the same: "A Time for Choosing," it would eventually come to be known. But Reagan just called it The Speech as he rolled it out at Lions Clubs, Kiwanis meetings, chambers of commerce, and whatever other civic and business groups would have him . . . ideally, with a generous honorarium attached. He knew every word, every pause, every applause line, like he knew his own mother's name.

And she played a role here too. Nelle's stubborn optimism bubbled up from every line.

The Speech is where Ronald Reagan became a voice in national politics that could not be ignored, making the conservative case in a way that was unreservedly accessible and welcoming. That was something hardly any other righties of that era had managed to do. American conservatives had spent too much of the past three decades echoing the dour despondency of Herbert Hoover: *Things are getting worse. There's nothing we can do about it . . . other than complain and pine for the old days.* In The Speech, Reagan's can-do spirit positively glowed. The Speech was where he channeled the radical spirit of the Founding Fathers. It was where he called for a less intrusive federal government and a less bloated welfare state. Where he highlighted the latest threats to freedom at home and abroad. Where he delighted in pointing out the many absurdities of liberal and leftist orthodoxies that were then taking hold in California, Washington, and New York and on college campuses across America as the Vietnam War heated up and the sixties were becoming what the sixties soon became. The Speech was where Reagan did all that in such a cheerful, sensible, comprehensive way that his business banquet and convention hall audiences couldn't help but conclude, *That Reagan guy sure seems to be having a wonderful time up there!*

No one was calling him the "happy warrior" yet. But the term certainly applied.

The Speech became such a popular attraction on what Reagan liked to call the "mashed potato circuit," Republican Party leaders sought him out in the heat of the 1964 presidential campaign. The race wasn't going so well for Barry Goldwater. Would Reagan craft a version of The Speech in support of the Republican nominee, who was on the way to getting clobbered by Lyndon Johnson less than a year after the assassination of John Kennedy? Reagan didn't hesitate. The Goldwater campaign bought a prime-time half hour on NBC.

"Ladies and gentlemen," the announcer intoned, "we take pride in presenting a thoughtful address by Ronald Reagan. Mr. Reagan?" And then it was pure, unadulterated Reagan. When his twenty-nine-minute presentation aired on October 27, a week before the election, it was the first time many Americans had ever heard someone talking about politics the way Reagan did that night. People were transfixed.

Before we get to what Reagan *said*, let's linger for a moment on *twenty-nine minutes*. The has-been movie actor and former television host spoke for twenty-nine uninterrupted minutes on national TV. Just him. No fancy graphics. No video B-roll. No Q&A. Just a man at a podium, talking sense to America, in front of a very polite, invited studio audience. It's almost impossible to imagine something like that in today's short-attention-span politics. Actual ideas, coherently developed, illustrated by precise statistics and historical quotes. In today's age of thirty-second TV spots and 140-character tweets . . . almost unthinkable. But this was 1964, and this was Ronald Reagan.

I'm not going to quote the whole thing, though I'm tempted to. It's that good. Just enough to make the point that The Speech was the official unveiling of what became known as Reagan's oratorical style. Notice the liberal use (if you'll excuse the term) of human anecdotes using snippets from the lives of individuals to make larger policy points. Those mini-stories would soon become a Reagan trademark. The Speech is generously flavored with them. A Cuban refugee warning his American friends about the many threats to freedom. A farmer in Arkansas whose land is auctioned off by U.S. marshals after agriculture bureaucrats accuse him of overplanting his rice allotment. A city in Ohio where "a million-and-a-half-dollar building completed only three years ago must be destroyed to make way for what government officials call a 'more compatible use of the land,'" which turns out to be a housing project. Inevitably, Reagan's critics would pick apart these tales, trying to find factual inaccuracies. *Let 'em!* Reagan knew the strength of a human story well told. It could stand up to whatever the nitpickers threw at it. The point was the point, and Reagan understood exactly how to make it.

Many of these anecdotes were his lighthearted way of skewering mushy-headed liberal Democrats, his favorite foil, the men and women he used to share a party with. Like this zinger: "We have so many people who can't see a fat man standing beside a thin one without coming to the conclusion the fat man got that way by taking advantage of the thin one."

Then there were the applause lines.

"The trouble with our liberal friends," Reagan says, "is not that they're ignorant. It's just that they know so much that isn't so." That became one of his most quoted lines ever. Quintessential Reagan.

"There's no argument over the choice between peace and war.

But there's only one guaranteed way you can have peace and you can have it in the next second. Surrender."

Another gem.

There's a reason those are called applause lines. When people heard them, in the hall and even at home, they couldn't help but clap their hands in agreement. These weren't political arguments in the usual sense. They were aimed at the heart as much as the head. Almost anyone could relate to insights like, "If we lose freedom here, there's no place to escape to. This is the last stand on earth."

That would remain a Reagan theme for the next half century: America as the world's last, best hope. How could you not clap at lines like those, delivered in Reagan's folksy style, with a small head shake and a glint in his eye? Firmly rooted in conservatism, he could give voice to patriotic themes that most Americans were comfortable embracing—and not make them sound scary. If he could make the long journey across the broad partisan divide, he said without quite saying it, couldn't anyone?

In those tight twenty-nine minutes, he never strayed far from his immediate agenda, boosting the Republican nominee for president. Whatever larger points he was making, he kept bringing them back to Goldwater. If 1964 was a time for choosing, Reagan said the election came down to a profoundly important choice: "Whether we believe in our capacity for self-government or whether we abandon the American revolution and confess that a little intellectual elite in a far-distant capitol can plan our lives for us better than we can plan them ourselves."

Who wanted that? Hardly anybody.

* * *

The Speech didn't get Barry Goldwater elected. It was already too late for that (though Reagan's address did raise one million last-minute dollars for the Goldwater-for-president campaign). The real Republican winner of 1964 was ... *Ronald Reagan.*

David S. Broder, the national-politics dean at the *Washington Post*, called Reagan's talk "the most successful national political debut since William Jennings Bryan electrified the 1896 Democratic Convention with his 'Cross of Gold' speech." I wasn't there for the '96 convention—not *1896*. So I'll go with Broder's recollection, if that's what it was. My memory of Reagan's speech is a little murky too. I was two years old in 1964. But I've studied this obsessively. And I can say with confidence that, in late October of that year, the American conservative movement found both its voice and its future. And it wouldn't be much longer until millions of other Americans caught on to Ronald Reagan too.

He was just different from the others ... before or since. Love him or hate him, there was no denying he was real.

How many politicians are wishy-washy when it comes to their proposals, policies, and partnerships? How many will say whatever they think the audience wants to hear, regardless of their own opinions? How many will stay silent when they should speak? Too many, too many, and too many. Reagan was something else. He wasn't just eloquent and authentic. He spoke with a clarity of convictions that came from deep research, real-world experience, and lifelong values. Because his message would inevitably take power and influence from the moderate Republicans who still dominated the party at that time, his vision was (to use a word more associated with Communists) truly subversive. Americans would see over time whether his upstart political movement would fundamentally change the Republican Party or melt like a snowball in July. But, given Reagan's patience and optimism (thanks, Nelle!), no one could possibly bet against him.

Another thing Reagan had going for him was that he was not obstinate in the manner of, say, a Capitol Hill ideologue whose objective is not to make a deal but to crush the other side. When Goldwater was trounced by Johnson, Reagan didn't kick over the sandcastle and storm off with his beach toys. He proudly stayed a Republican. He was in it for the long haul. He believed that good things come to those who wait. (Thanks for that, too, Nelle!)

Soon enough, Republican Party honchos in California were asking if Reagan would consider running for governor in 1966 against Pat Brown, a two-term liberal Democrat who was already making plans for term number three. Reagan happily agreed to go for it. Then Brown got cute during the primary season, helping to undermine Reagan's more moderate Republican opponent, former San Francisco mayor George Christopher. Brown figured the ex-actor rookie candidate would be much easier to beat.

Bad bet.

As the vote grew near, Reagan narrowed his pitch to two issues that were infuriating Californians that fall—and not just hardcore conservatives. He promised to "clean up the mess at Berkeley," where student protesters were running wild on the state university campus, and "send the welfare bums back to work." Governor

Brown would never talk so plainly or dare to offend his own elite backers. He was so desperate at the end, he aired one of the sleaziest political commercials of all time, which totally backfired. The TV ad showed Brown talking to two Black girls and saying, "You know I'm running against an actor." When the schoolgirls nod, he continues: "You know who shot Abraham Lincoln, don't you? An actor shot Lincoln." In the end, the race wasn't even close. Reagan was the fresh voice. Brown sounded like more of the same. Reagan strolled to victory on November 8, 1966, with better than 57 percent of the vote.

And then came the hard part for any politician: actually doing the job he'd just been elected to do.

However tumultuous the late sixties would become in the rest of America, they'd be even more so in California. The militant Black Panther Party would burst out of gritty Oakland. The hippies' Summer of Love would flower first in San Francisco's Haight-Ashbury district. No campus would symbolize student unrest like the University of California at Berkeley. Watts in Los Angeles would become the quintessentially riotous urban ghetto. And Bobby Kennedy's assassination at L.A.'s Ambassador Hotel, less than a year and a half into Reagan's governorship, would put an exclamation point on all of it. The world was changing in unpredictable ways, and Californians had plenty of reasons to feel anxious about it. Their newly elected conservative governor certainly had his hands full. But Reagan wasn't the kind of politician who was satisfied making grand proclamations on the campaign trail, then stalling out as soon as he got into office. His version of conservatism very much included achieving stuff. And he'd been around long enough to know that obstinacy and rigidity were rarely the best ways to get meaningful things done.

Yes, he'd won a commanding victory against the out-of-gas liberal Democrat Pat Brown. Yes, he had the backing of old-guard Hollywood (Bob Hope, Jack Benny, Dinah Shore, George Burns, James Cagney, Jimmy Stewart, and John Wayne), as well as some brand-name California capitalists such as A. C. "Cy" Rubel (oil), Holmes Tuttle (cars), Alfred Bloomingdale (department stores), Leonard Firestone (tires), and Justin Dart Sr. (drugstores). But California was still California. It wasn't Dixon, Illinois, even if a Midwest-bred conservative now had the big office in Sacramento.

High on Reagan's list of priorities were tax cuts. He'd said during the campaign—and believed in his heart—that families and businesses in California were being choked by a smog of taxes, especially property taxes, which almost everyone seemed to hate. But with Democrats in firm control of the state legislature, Reagan knew he couldn't just wave a magic tax cut wand. He had to make some kind of deal with assembly Speaker Jesse Unruh. The Speaker had such a grip on his fellow Democrats, they had a nickname for him, which they mostly used without a smirk. He was Big Daddy Unruh, and he was rarely disobeyed. With a very Reagan combination of personal charm and logical argument, the new governor got Unruh to agree to a freeze in government hiring and a nice-size property tax cut. In California! It didn't come free. In exchange, Unruh got something too. He got to hike the sales tax from 3 to

5 percent, the booze tax from $1.50 to $2 a gallon, and the cigarette tax from 3 to 10 cents a pack. But Reagan got the cut he really cared about, and people didn't *have to* smoke or drink. And both men got to boast that they'd balanced the state budget.

Sometimes, Reagan understood, you have to give to get. The trick is compromising shrewdly without giving up your core beliefs.

So, was the property tax cut a conservative victory? Yes, a partial one, but still worth celebrating, especially for struggling middle-class homeowners, the core of the Reagan constituency. And Reagan learned a practical lesson about politics: you can always stay pure and get nothing if that's what you're aiming for. But it's often better to get something, even if the price is a certain amount of compromise. Despite his reputation as a staunch conservative, Governor Reagan was always open to sensible compromise. And he never surrendered the conservative principle that the burden of government is often too high. He was still the governor fighting for lower taxes, and he'd fight that fight again the next time he got the chance. But he'd rather get something for Californians than nothing at all.

Reagan faced similar choices on a wide array of issues, over and over again, during his two four-year terms as governor. How rigid he was or how flexible—well, it all depended on the issue and how much leeway he felt like he had. He had plenty, it turned out, when it came to the state university system and the student radicals who thought they were in charge. Reagan laid down the law on that one, and he refused to budge.

Public disgust at the spoiled protesters had been bubbling up for a couple of years. It grew only worse as the radicals took over administrative buildings, shut down state campuses, and clashed violently with the police. As unruly as the students were, some faculty and administrators were almost as irresponsible. They refused to stand up to the loudmouths and let the learning resume. Delivering on a key campaign promise, Reagan appointed several new members to the University of California Board of Regents, who promptly booted the system's hapless president, Clark Kerr. When protesters took over People's Park in Berkeley, Reagan sent in the California Highway Patrol and the California National Guard, whose troops occupied the city for a full two weeks. Despite the liberal hand-wringing and howls of student outrage, order was restored.

That didn't put an end to student protests in California. Nothing could have done that. But it sent a loud and clear message to the troublemakers: have whatever opinions you want to, but Governor Reagan won't tolerate violence or disruption. That clear message made Reagan a villain to some in the so-called youth movement and their cheerleaders in the national media. But just as he expected, his hard line won applause from the vast majority of Californians. They shared his "old-fashioned" view: schools are for learning, and they should stay that way. The people stood with their no-nonsense governor against the spoiled brats.

By then, national Republicans were already thinking about the 1968 presidential race. Was it any surprise that the name of the first-term governor of California soon ended up in the mix? He certainly hadn't paid his dues yet. He hadn't had time. Richard Nixon, Nelson Rockefeller, Michigan governor George Romney, Ohio governor James Rhodes—they'd all been laying careful groundwork. But

Reagan's governorship was off to such a rousing start, he quickly emerged as a leading alternative if neither of the two front-runners, Nixon and Rockefeller, scored a first-ballot win at the convention in Miami Beach. In the end, Nixon had the delegates, twenty-five more than he needed to seal the nomination. So Reagan would have to wait. But it was still quite an accomplishment: less than halfway through his first term as governor, people were already floating the idea of "President Reagan."

That's what happens when you remain authentic and know where to take your shots. When to compromise, when to hang tough. That December, a month after Nixon beat Hubert Humphrey for the White House, Reagan was chosen by his peers to chair the Republican Governors Association. It was a consolation prize but still a nice one. And he won reelection in 1970 against Jesse Unruh, the Democratic assembly Speaker he'd negotiated tax cuts with. The labor unions, the public school teachers, and some of the citizen groups lined up for the Democrat. But a majority of the voters said yes this time to four more years.

There are parts of Reagan's record as governor, in his first and second terms, that can appear distinctly liberal in hindsight. He ushered in California's strongest gun control law up to that time. He signed a bill that vastly expanded legal abortion. Though he was a staunch supporter of capital punishment, he managed to impose it only once in eight years. Some of Reagan's critics like to point to these facts as evidence that maybe he wasn't quite as conservative as history now portrays him.

But here's the thing: context. Every one of these situations has to be seen in context. Reagan was never a strict ideologue. He always had a strong practical side. He believed in what worked and what could be accomplished, the reason he was always open to the notion of sensible compromise. And when you take a closer look at some of these political surprises, there's almost always more to the story than the down-and-dirty headlines at first suggest.

Take the gun issue, for example. Reagan wasn't taking aim at the Second Amendment. He was responding to a grave public concern about militant Black Panthers walking around with loaded guns. After twenty-six Panthers, some of them armed, burst into the state capitol and were arrested for disrupting the proceedings, the legislature passed a law that prohibited civilians from carrying firearms in public and Reagan signed it. He also signed a fifteen-day cooling-off period before someone could buy a handgun. Those were, indeed, two of the state's strongest gun control measures ever. But times were different then, and so was the gun debate.

He came out in favor of another bill that protected doctors from criminal prosecution for performing abortions in hospitals. The bill was supported by the American Medical Association, the American Bar Association, the American Academy of Pediatrics, the California Medical Association, the California Bar Association—even Reagan's own father-in-law, Dr. Loyal Davis. But wait! Reagan changed his mind after consulting with James Cardinal McIntyre, the Catholic archbishop of Los Angeles. His Eminence convinced Reagan to veto the bill since it allowed abortions in the case of birth defects, and that gave the legislators pause. It was only after the lawmakers agreed to drop the birth defect language that Reagan signed the abortion bill, decriminalizing the procedure to keep doctors out of jail.

In the years to come, of course, Reagan would grow staunchly right-to-life and would win the enthusiastic backing of many anti-abortion groups. He later said he regretted signing that California abortion bill. He said he'd been too new in his own journey to fully grasp its implications.

Live and learn . . . and compromise to make things better. That was always the Reagan way.

CHAPTER 7

BIGGER TENT

As Reagan eyed the White House, he understood: he'd
never get there if all he did was cater to the people who
already loved him. By teaming up with former opponents, he could broaden his appeal, heighten his chance
of victory, and deepen his impact.

LESSON LEARNED: YES, YOU CAN COMPROMISE
WITHOUT BEING COMPROMISED.

Try and try again.

It had been eight years since Ronald Reagan's first run for president, if you can call it that, in 1968, and it wasn't really his idea
that time. When Nixon turned out to be much stronger than the
Reagan whisperers had imagined and the Republican convention
didn't need to be brokered at all, the first-term California governor
looked like he might have been reaching a little beyond his grasp.

Compared to that early flirtation with national politics, the
1976 presidential campaign was the real deal. It didn't turn out
any more successfully, meaning Reagan didn't win the Republican

97

nomination this time, either. But he proved he could go toe to toe with anyone. He established himself as *the* leading voice—not just *a* leading voice—of American conservatism. And he earned his place high on the short list of serious Republican contenders in any future race for president.

The timing is important here. All this was in the shadow of Watergate. Nixon was driven from office on August 9, 1974, and replaced by his appointed vice president, Gerald Ford. Ford pardoned Nixon and was now running for a full term of his own. Reagan jumped into the race on November 20, 1975, with a full-blown campaign this time. Challenging an incumbent—even one who'd never been elected to the job—came with some special challenges. The main one was that almost all the political experts just assumed that Ford already had the nomination sewn up. Not since Lyndon Johnson in 1968 had an incumbent failed to win the backing of his own party, and Ford was a perfectly genial guy, hard to hate *personally*. But John Sears, Reagan's savvy campaign manager, had a plan, and it made a certain amount of sense: throw everything they had at the early primaries and caucuses. If they could win just a couple of those, they really might dislodge the presumption that Ford had the Republican nomination in the bag. And once the bubble of inevitability was popped, Reagan could out-talk, out-charm, and out-run the accidental president.

Not a bad strategy, as long shots go.

For Reagan, the timing was just about ideal. He'd left 'em smiling in California, having shifted the state's political culture significantly to the right. He could have gone for a third term as governor but was happy to move on. He was a big draw again on his beloved (and increasingly lucrative) mashed-potato circuit with his latest, updated version of The Speech. Only now he could also test-drive his best new lines in front of a different focus group every night, seeing what might work in a presidential campaign. For him, those appearances were like the spring training Cubs games he used to broadcast in Des Moines. His rhetorical lineup would be ready by Opening Day. He was, to use a phrase that had once been applied to Richard Nixon, "tanned, rested, and ready." Reagan hit the ground running that fall.

"Today," he said quite plainly on launch day, "it is difficult to find leaders who are independent of the forces that have brought us our problems—the Congress, the bureaucracy, the lobbyists, big business and big labor. If America is to survive and go forward, this must change. It will only change when the American people vote for a leadership that listens to them, relies on them, and seeks to return government to them. We need a government that is confident not of what *it* can do, but of what the people can do."

There it was: Reagan's welcoming version of conservatism, suspicious of big government, his faith planted firmly in the people.

He chose villains who had consistently worked for him. Campus radicals. Welfare chiselers. Corrupt labor leaders. Clueless bureaucrats. The Communists in charge of China and the Soviet Union and their expansionist intent. He championed the regular, middle-class folks who were groaning under the burden of paying for everything. And he always talked about the hope for better days ahead. Out on the campaign trail in New Hampshire, Florida, and the other early-primary states, Reagan's optimistic conservatism, a combination he now seemed to own, connected easily with voters—

and not just the hard right-wingers. Next to Reagan's feisty phrases and good-natured humor, Ford's muddled moderation was just ... *blah*. Addressing crowds and interacting with voters, Reagan was the one with the sizzle, even though the clunkier Ford still had all the institutional advantages of the White House. There's nothing quite like arriving in New Hampshire on Air Force One. But often, it seemed, Reagan was already on the ground when the big plane landed, winning hearts and minds one by one by one.

Maybe not enough of them. Only the primaries would determine that. But the former governor of California was giving the accidental president a real race. Whoever won the Democratic nomination—Jimmy Carter? Jerry Brown? Mo Udall?—would surely campaign on change, saying the country needed a whole new direction to shake off the lingering hangover of Watergate. And yet ... Reagan could offer a new direction, too, without all the big-government liberalism that many Americans were growing weary of.

That was the pitch, anyway.

As the primary season was about to begin, the Ford campaign seemed concerned about Reagan's obvious popularity. The president told reporters that Reagan was "too far to the right" to guide the nation into the future.

"I don't see how anyone could be a right-wing extremist and win two elections by landslide margins in California," Reagan countered. But that wasn't the best part of his comeback. When reporters asked him to address the dig, Reagan responded: "I am a little surprised about his statement about my so-called extremism. It does come rather strange because he tried on two different occasions to persuade me to accept any of several cabinet positions in his administration."

The Ford campaign was forced to admit that was true.

Reagan lost the Iowa caucuses and the New Hampshire primary, but both contests were squeakers, far too close for comfort at the Ford campaign. Ford also prevailed in the next two competitive primaries, Florida (by a little) and Illinois (by a lot). But just as the experts were taking bows for their prescience, Reagan won a surprise upset in North Carolina, thanks to a strong assist from Senator Jesse Helms, then proceeded to win a string of states: Georgia, Indiana, Nebraska, Arkansas, Idaho, Nevada, and, most importantly, Texas, where he carried all twenty-four congressional districts. The expected Ford blowout hadn't blown yet. And it wouldn't. But Ford bounced back in his native Michigan and quite a few other states. And as the primary season staggered to the end, the incumbent president appeared to be nailing down a small but solid lead.

Then came the eleventh-hour twist. A very *Reagan* twist.

On July 27, less than three weeks before the delegates were set to assemble in Kansas City for the Republican National Convention, Reagan made a surprise announcement. He had asked liberal Republican senator Richard Schweiker of Pennsylvania to be his running mate. As the *New York Times* put it the next morning: "Mr. Reagan reached all the way across the country and the party spectrum in naming the 50-year-old, two-term Senator, one of the most liberal and pro-labor Republican voices in Congress."

Just because Reagan was a principled conservative, that didn't mean he couldn't team up with a fellow Republican who had a different outlook. And he saw no need to apologize for it. As far as he was concerned, he was simply enlarging the tent to welcome more voters in. "I have selected a man of independent thought with a background in business and sixteen years of public service," Reagan said when he broke the news. "He is respected by his colleagues, but he has not become a captive of what I call the Washington buddy system." A Reagan-Schweiker ticket, he said, was one "behind which all Republicans can unite and one which will lead our party to victory in November."

Some conservatives howled in outrage. How could the conservative Reagan embrace the liberal Schweiker? The word *betrayal* was thrown around. Reagan's big booster in North Carolina, Senator Helms, was spitting mad. He said Republicans ought to abandon Reagan and draft Conservative Party U.S. senator James L. Buckley of New York as the Republican nominee. That call went nowhere, but the Schweiker move revealed something key to Reagan's trademark approach: Be a conservative. Stick to your principles. But don't be stubborn about it. Build coalitions where you have to. Reach across the aisle or the ideological divide if that will improve the chance of victory. You can't achieve anything if you lose.

That winning philosophy is totally lost on many in today's Republican Party. Led by Donald Trump, their philosophy is to divide, exclude, and anger—then use that anger to juice turnout just enough (or not) to eke out a win.

That's not an approach that expands a party or unites a country. Reagan preferred to win.

The trick, he understood, was compromising without being

compromised, being open-minded without alienating the core conservative base. It was a bit of a tightrope walk that time. It always would be. And it wouldn't always work. But Reagan's willingness to try was one of the things that set him apart from the downcast conservatives who, for the sake of purity, were resigned to losing year after year after year. We've seen that pattern repeatedly with Trump's leadership and the resulting losses in 2018, 2020, and 2022. Reagan had also seen that with some of the purists in the Goldwater campaign. It wasn't a pattern he intended to follow or a mistake he planned to repeat.

The Schweiker move wasn't enough to outrun Ford's incumbency. Ford crossed the finish line with 1,187 delegates to Reagan's 1,070. Ford chose Senator Bob Dole as his running mate, and Reagan didn't hold a grudge. He delivered that rousing speech on the floor of the convention in Kansas City, the one that made me declare to my parents, "I'm a Republican." He went right back out on the road and campaigned for the Republican ticket in twenty states, making sure he left a good taste even in the mouths of Republicans who'd supported the sitting president all along. He let other people say what he clearly must have thought: that if he'd had a one-on-one shot at Jimmy Carter that November, he could have closed the deal in a way that Jerry Ford was unable to. Change—conservative change—might finally have saved the day.

But that was all speculation. There was no way of knowing for sure. This much, however, was certain: in a funny way, Reagan still won. Just as he'd been the real Republican winner of the 1964 campaign (Goldwater was finished, Reagan had just begun), so was he the Republican winner of 1976. After his defeat by Carter, Ford

---

was done politically. Though Reagan failed to win the Republican nomination this time, his charisma and clarity of vision—and, yes, his willingness to reach across the party's ideological divide—left a strong impression on many voters, including a lot of former or restive Democrats. They liked his openness. They liked his optimism. They liked his big-tent approach.

And 1980 was just four years away.

When Reagan lost to Ford, he very easily could have said, *Thank you very much,* and promptly faded away. He was sixty-five years old, the retirement age for many Americans. He'd been a sportscaster, a movie star, a TV host, a popular public speaker, a union chief, a two-term governor, and a serious presidential candidate. He'd certainly had a full career. And let's state the obvious: losing is never fun in politics, even for someone who wasn't expected to win. No matter how the odds are stacked against you, you always psych yourself into believing *Maybe I can pull it off this time!* After Ford got his eviction notice and Jimmy Carter moved into 1600 Pennsylvania Avenue, Reagan had every right to retreat to his ranch and, literally, ride off into the sunset. It wouldn't have been such a bad life. Relaxing with Nancy and his four grown children. Putting in some saddle time and catching up on the chores. Maybe sitting on a corporate board or two. Taking the long view on whatever issues came up.

Well, *no.*

Despite his age and his crowded résumé, Reagan wasn't anywhere close to calling it quits. He didn't believe for a second that his political career was over. Call it resilience. Call it perseverance.

Call it whatever you like. He was looking forward, not back. By the time the dust had settled on the 1976 election, he and his political advisors were already eyeing 1980. And the best way to position himself for that, he decided, was to offer a frank and continuing assessment of Jimmy Carter's presidency. Reagan would, to put it another way, become the first-term Democrat's number one critic from the right. In real time. Who was better positioned for that role than Ronald Reagan? Ex-president Ford wasn't going to do it. He took the elder-statesman path that Reagan eschewed: long days on the golf course, ponderous university speeches, and a 454-page memoir titled *A Time to Heal.* Leave the nostalgia and the navel-gazing to Ford. Reagan chose to stay engaged on the front lines of American politics.

And that's exactly what he did.

In speeches and interviews and newspaper columns and radio broadcasts and whatever other forums came along, he shared his day-by-day analysis of the policy blunders, political foibles, and incompetence that characterized the presidency of the former governor of Georgia. Reagan never attacked Carter personally except in the gentlest ways. How could he? Carter was a plainly decent man. He just lacked the leadership qualities and political skills to move America in the right direction, and he was tied to a party of narrow-interest groups that had lost touch with the needs and desires of regular Americans. And Carter kept doing things Reagan found boneheaded.

Pardoning Vietnam-era draft evaders. Declaring energy conservation the "moral equivalent of war." Shifting the main focus of American foreign policy from anti-communism to human rights.

Opposing the B-1 bomber. Giving up U.S. control of the Panama Canal. And that was just Carter's first year in office.

Reagan's critiques of these particular issues aren't important anymore. They seem fleeting, looking back. But taken together, his play-by-play analysis of the Democratic administration helped to seal Reagan's position as the Republican to beat in 1980. And at the same time he was opining on the issues of the day, he was also offering a broader analysis of the future of the conservative movement and the Republican Party. For one thing, he argued strongly that the GOP was still the right home for conservatives, contradicting some purists on the right who wanted to go off and create a new party of some sort. He also spoke passionately about the importance of attracting disaffected Democrats and independents, particularly in the South and Midwest. The Democratic Party, once the voice and the home of working-class Americans, had lost its way, he was convinced. In Reagan's view, the Democrats had been captured by a tax-and-spend addiction and the very forces he had long been railing against: campus radicals (now in their thirties and beyond), union bosses (in government employee unions, especially), and civil rights activists who'd moved way past demanding equal opportunity and now wanted equal results.

With the Democrats so far to the left, Reagan argued, Republican conservatism really was the majority philosophy of America now. He made that point explicitly when he accepted an invitation to appear before a rapt audience of fellow conservatives at the 1977 gathering of the Conservative Political Action Committee (CPAC): "Despite what some in the press may say, we who are proud to call ourselves 'conservative' are not a minority of a minority party. We are part of the great majority of Americans of both major parties and of most of the independents as well."

He said he understood that the American Right included "economic conservatives" and "social conservatives," people who embraced the small-government philosophy with different emphases. But he asked: "Isn't it possible to combine the two major segments of contemporary American conservatism into one politically effective whole?"

His answer was . . . *Absolutely.*

And without quite saying it, he made clear who could lead that unified national party into the brightly lit future it so obviously deserved. "We went a long way toward doing it in California," he told the CPACers that day. "We can do it in America. This is not a dream, a wistful hope. It is and has been a reality. I have seen the conservative future and it works."

In Jimmy Carter, Ronald Reagan had something that was missing when he took on Gerald Ford.

A perfect foil.

A sitting president from the other party who couldn't make his own luck and, even when it seemed he might, couldn't catch a break.

As Carter's term rolled on, lots of things got worse. Almost nothing got better. Economic stagnation. Long lines at gas stations. Sky-high inflation and interest rates. An expansionist Soviet Union. A revived Cold War. In January 1979, after Iran's pro-American leader Mohammad Reza Shah Pahlavi fled the country, Ayatollah

Ruhollah Khomeini ended his fourteen-year exile in France and returned to Iran to establish an Islamic republic. That couldn't be good. Carter sunk deeper and deeper into the quicksand of starry-eyed liberalism and inadequate leadership.

He got a much-deserved boost in March 1979 when Israel's Menachem Begin and Egypt's Anwar Sadat signed a peace treaty they'd negotiated the year before at Camp David with Carter's deep involvement. But the glow didn't last. On July 15, the beleaguered president delivered a televised address that highlighted what he called a "crisis of confidence" among the American people (his "malaise" speech). It turned out that the main thing Americans lacked confidence in was their president. Carter's approval rating had fallen so low—below 20 percent—that even his fellow Democrats saw him as deeply vulnerable. Why else would he draw primary challenges from the likes of Ted Kennedy and Jerry Brown? Carter's shaky position grew even shakier on November 4 when the Khomeini regime allowed Islamist students and radicals to raid the U.S. embassy in Tehran and hold fifty-two Americans hostage.

Almost anything could happen next.

Reagan wasn't the only high-profile Republican itching for a shot at Carter in 1980. Former CIA director and Republican National Committee chairman George Bush, Illinois congressman John Anderson, Tennessee senator Howard Baker, Illinois congressman Phil Crane, former treasury secretary John Connally, and Kansas senator Bob Dole all raised their hands and asked, *Why not me?* But Reagan, who'd come so close the last time and had stayed very much in the game, was leading in all the polls—so much so that campaign manager John Sears urged an "above-the-fray" strategy. Reagan skipped many of the multicandidate forums in the summer and fall of 1979, letting the other candidates slice each other up while he maintained a tone of tolerant distance.

Once the voting started, Bush got a glimmer of hope when he snuck past Reagan in the Iowa straw poll, giving him "the Big Mo," he claimed. With Reagan ignoring the Puerto Rican primary, Bush won there too. But Reagan romped in New Hampshire, and he barely looked back from there, lengthening his lead almost every week after that. The intraparty drama was a distant memory by the time the delegates arrived in Detroit for the convention, where Reagan could have chosen almost anyone he wanted as his vice presidential candidate.

Perhaps another prominent figure from the party's conservative wing?

A name that would tickle the old guard, who'd been waiting for this day since they nominated Barry Goldwater in 1964?

No way. Not Reagan. Not his style.

In a move that could now fairly be called *Reaganesque*, he went in precisely the opposite direction. He reached across the party in a different way than he had before. He offered the job to his strongest primary-season opponent, the defeated Republican candidate who could hardly have been any more different from the folksy conservative icon who was now enlisting him.

George H. W. Bush.

East Coast origins. Ivy League education. Republican royalty. Inherited power and wealth. Politically moderate. Bush was almost the flip side of Ronald Reagan, right down to the double initials that were planted like twin geraniums in the middle of his name. The two men had never been close. Why would they be? But Reagan chose Bush—and for all the usual Reagan reasons. He knew he already had the hard-core conservatives, economic, social, and hybrid. He knew the election in November would hang on the vast middle of America, far more than the Republican primaries had. Moderates. Former Democrats. Independents. Suburbanites. People who didn't spend all day long obsessed with politics because they were too busy living their lives. Reagan worried he'd come up short if all he did was super-serve the people who already loved him. There just weren't enough of them, even if their numbers had been swelling during the Carter years. The road to victory was a six-lane highway, Reagan believed—not a narrow path. And it could certainly be helpful having a running mate who played to a different crowd.

To Reagan, it really didn't matter if he had to hold his nose. Picking Bush was just his latest chance to display his deep resilience and his openness to tactical compromises in support of a larger cause. Bush had qualities that Reagan didn't. Experience. Connections. An appeal to some voters who might be worried about Reagan's distance from the ways of Washington, his Hollywood heritage, or his "cowboy" foreign policy instincts. One good thing about picking someone different from yourself: you get a built-in counterweight.

From his days in Hollywood and Sacramento, Reagan had learned the importance of building solid coalitions if you want to get things done. Yes, sometimes you do have to compromise. Over time, Reagan had grown more deft at building alliances and more confident that he could maintain his own principles and values, even when some of the people around him had different ones. And honestly, it made life more interesting to trade ideas.

Getting elected, Reagan understood, meant compromising with someone else, Bush in this case. And it also meant compromising with himself. In his head, Reagan was still deeply planted in the conservative tradition. In his heart, he didn't feel a natural bond with American aristocrats like the Bushes. But in the end Reagan was confident enough and ambitious enough to burst the bubble, to break the seal, to go outside his comfort zone—pick whichever analogy you like. He was willing to risk averse reactions from his longtime allies.

Jimmy Carter campaigned hard that fall. He emphasized his role as a peacemaker in a dangerous world, highlighting the Camp David Accords and the international coalition he assembled when the Soviet Union invaded Afghanistan, which led to a massive boycott of the 1980 Summer Olympics in Moscow. He charged that Reagan's version of anti-communism was stuck in a bygone era and warned that a Republican victory in November would threaten civil rights and social programs that went all the way back to the New Deal. He poked at Reagan's support for supply-side economics, noting that George Bush, Reagan's own running mate, had derided the concept as "voodoo economics."

For his part, Reagan kept delivering his message in his usual, down-to-earth way, taking his shots at Carter with a shrug and a smile. Instead of getting into the weeds on supply-side tax policy, he added a fresh line to an old quip from the lecture circuit: "A recession is when your neighbor loses his job. A depression is when you lose yours. And recovery is when Jimmy Carter loses *his*."

Asked about his own TV commercials, Reagan offered: "I heard the other day they have one for Jimmy Carter. It's called, 'The Best of the Carter Years.' It's a three-second station break." When Carter lit into Reagan as a threat to the future of humanity, he responded thusly: "The President lately has been saying that I am irresponsible. And you know, I'll admit to that if he'll confess he's *responsible*."

When Carter and Reagan met for their sole one-on-one debate, in Cleveland a week before Election Day, 80.6 million people tuned in, the most in American history. But it wasn't *this* issue or *that* issue that most people remembered from that night. It was a phrase of Reagan's. When Carter said that Reagan began his political career by opposing Medicare, Reagan responded with a head shake and a wink. "There you go again," he said, before explaining that he had supported an alternate program for providing senior health care. "I happened to favor the other piece of legislation and thought that it would be better for the senior citizens and provide better care than the one that was finally passed," he said.

But it was the four-word phrase that lingered . . . and Reagan's dead-on delivery: "There you go again."

It wasn't a clean sweep for Ronald Reagan on November 4, 1980. Not quite. Jimmy Carter won six states and the District of Columbia. But Reagan received the highest number of electoral votes, 489 of 538, ever won by a nonincumbent presidential candidate. Compare that to what Donald Trump called a "massive landslide victory" of 366 electoral votes in 2016. (Trump has not only downsized our ambitions. He has downsized even our victories.) And Reagan had some very long coattails. That night Republicans picked up twelve seats in the U.S. Senate, winning control of the chamber for the first time since 1954. Though Democrats retained a majority in the House of Representatives, Republicans added thirty-four seats there. Republicans also picked up four governorships.

Reagan's combination of conservative principle, appealing personality, and willingness to compromise produced a conservative realignment in American politics that commentators were soon calling the "Reagan Revolution."

All its namesake had to do now was govern. And really, how hard could that be?

CHAPTER 8

KITCHEN CABINET

As the new president got to work, he was surrounded by talented cabinet secretaries and agency heads, who all had strong opinions but couldn't seem to get along. It was Reagan's old pals from California who really had his ear.

LESSON LEARNED:
THERE IS NO "US VERSUS THEM" IN TEAM.

Ronald and Nancy Reagan didn't move to Washington immediately after the election. They stayed back in California for a few weeks, getting ready for all that awaited them and consulting with the members of the former governor's "kitchen cabinet."

Who else were they going to turn to at such a crucial time?

This small circle of loyal friends and backers had been at Reagan's side since the 1960s. Emphasis on *loyal*. These were the people who'd encouraged Reagan to run for governor in the first place and had helped to fund his two statewide races. They played the same key role when he started thinking about running for president. They were there for all three national campaigns, providing encouragement and direction and, not inconsequentially, bringing in other generous donors. Like Reagan, most of them were self-made millionaires who'd found success out west and developed an interest in politics along the way. Sharing their friend's conservative philosophy and eager to advance his prominence, they'd always been a valuable source of ideas and a reliable sounding board. And Reagan's kitchen cabinet was more than a phone tree. From time to time they all got together to hash out the issues of the moment and give their friend, the governor, now the incoming president, their best guidance and advice. More than anyone else, these were Reagan's peers and his closest confidants.

There was car dealer Holmes Tuttle. Oil tool executive William A. Wilson. Builder Marts of America chairman Thomas A. Roe. Beer baron Joseph Coors. Lawyers Charles Z. Wick, William French Smith, and Edwin Meese. Drugstore mogul Justin Dart was the informal head of the group, which also included department store executive Alfred Bloomingdale, whose wife, Betsy, was one of Nancy's closest friends. A few others came and went. But the Bloomingdales were so excited about Reagan's victory, they promptly took an apartment at the famous Watergate complex in Washington so they'd be available to their good friends around the clock.

As Reagan began considering people for important jobs in the new administration, he sought the advice of the members of the kitchen cabinet. Of course he did, and of course they were more than happy to oblige, floating the names of like-minded conservatives they thought would fit well on the Reagan team. That included quite a few prospects who'd made their reputations in places far, far from Washington.

Not surprisingly, some Washington Republicans found all this a bit too cozy for comfort. The kitchen cabinet was fine, they allowed, as long as Reagan's political universe extended from Sacramento to L.A. But now that he'd be moving into the White House and had a whole country to run . . . well, wouldn't he need people around him who were wise in the ways of Washington? That's what the capital denizens kept saying.

That sentiment, which was quite pervasive in the power halls of D.C., was easy enough to parody: *What about us?* they all seemed to ask. But the more Reagan thought about it, the more he grew convinced that the insiders might have a point.

As he began to assemble his new team, no position was more important than White House chief of staff. That person, whoever it was, would run the day-to-day business of the office of the president. The operational people, the administrative staff, the congressional liaisons, the communications team—they'd all report to the chief of staff. Even the cabinet members would be beholden. Before anyone or anything got into the Oval Office, he, she, or it would need to go through the chief of staff.

Almost everyone—certainly everyone in California—assumed the job would go to longtime Reagan advisor and kitchen cabinet member Ed Meese. A moot court champion at the University of California law school and then a hard-driving assistant district attorney, Meese had served as Reagan's chief of staff in the governor's office, where he was instrumental in the crackdown on student protesters at People's Park in Berkeley. Meese had a special knack for explaining complex ideas to Reagan in Reagan's own language. "Reagan's geographer," reporter Lou Cannon once described him.

Following the 1980 Iowa caucuses, Meese had joined Reagan's presidential campaign full-time as chief of staff and senior issues advisor, a role that grew only larger with the ouster of campaign director John Sears. The morning after Election Day, Reagan named Meese to head his presidential transition team, which included several other members of his California kitchen cabinet. Going forward, everything seemed wired for Ed Meese. But the kitchen cabinet stalwart was in for an unpleasant surprise.

During the 1980 primary season, Reagan had been impressed with George Bush's campaign manager, James Baker—so impressed that, after picking Bush as his running mate, Reagan brought Baker into the fall campaign, asking him to work with Meese and campaign chairman William Casey. Baker was handed the high-profile duty of guiding Reagan's debate strategy. Again, Baker rose to the occasion ("There you go again") and left Reagan impressed. A Princeton-educated Houston lawyer who'd been Bush's regular tennis partner at the Houston Country Club, Baker was a deeply sourced Republican insider who'd gone on to serve in the Nixon administration and as Gerald Ford's undersecretary of commerce before managing Ford's 1976 campaign.

What he wasn't was a longtime Reagan *friend*. He'd never been part of the kitchen cabinet, like Meese and the others had. The Texan was *Bush's guy*, and Reagan had few warm feelings toward the Houston crowd. "Country club Republicans," the Californians sneered about these low-key insiders with their middle-of-the-road politics and, in the Bushes' case, significant ancestral wealth. And weren't they from the wing of the party that Reagan had just whipped in the primaries, thanks to his frankly conservative message and down-to-earth personality?

Yet Reagan named the insider's insider, the well-connected Baker, as his White House chief of staff. Ideals could guide your path, Reagan concluded, but someone needed to provide a trail map. It was the first time anyone could remember that the top position in the White House went to someone who'd run his primary opponent's campaign.

Ed Meese wasn't left entirely in the cold. He was named counselor to the president, a senior position that came with a seat in the cabinet and on the National Security Council. Several other California aides and friends got positions too. Deputy White House chief of staff went to Michael Deaver, a governor's office staffer who'd been especially attentive to Nancy. ("Nancy's Nancy," some of the Californians called Deaver behind his back, though he was also credited with performing the Heimlich maneuver when a peanut got stuck in Reagan's throat during a 1976 campaign flight.)

Together, Baker, Meese, and Deaver would be the "troika," the key White House staffers who would guide the new administration through its early days with some familiar faces in the mix. Lawyer and kitchen cabinet veteran Charles Wick went to the International Communications Agency. William Wilson became emissary to the Vatican. And a real plum, attorney general, went to California lawyer William French Smith. But Bush's guy Baker was over all of them. And once he came on board, he immediately began filling other slots with Bush and Ford moderates.

There was disappointment, even some audible grumbling, in

California and among movement conservatives. Some even spoke of betrayal. They'd been waiting a long time for this. But Reagan had realized he needed to live in the real world. And just like he'd chosen Bush to help him win in November, Reagan decided he needed Bush's guy to help him govern come Inauguration Day. It was not a compromise Reagan was eager to make. It was one he thought he *needed* to, and he was confident he could handle the blowback on the right. He'd built up strong credit among conservatives on his long march to the presidency, and he figured that would protect him. He also knew that his loyal supporters eagerly wanted him to succeed, even if they had to gulp hard like Reagan had done and make room for the Bushies. If that was the price of having Ronald Reagan in the White House, they could live with the fear of a Bush "coup," confident that Reagan would never let things drift too far to the middle or the left.

It's an incredibly rare human quality, the ability to see in your bitter rival the key to your own success. But Reagan had it, and his longtime supporters had enough faith in him to swallow the compromise their leader thought he had to make. Everyone understood, Reagan included: this was a marriage of convenience, just as the 1976 and 1980 tickets had been with the liberal Richard Schweiker and the moderate George Bush. While Reagan didn't love it, he had asked for it, and he was the one who eventually would have to make it work.

Reagan was a true conservative at heart. But as a governor, he understood the practical requirements of governing. He was confident enough, as Lincoln had been 120 years earlier, to surround himself with rivals and people of different ideology to help run the government and bring the country together. Despite the doubts of some, it would lead to unrivaled accomplishments at home and abroad. It would also lead to a forty-nine-state reelection victory. He could surround himself with different voices because he knew who was ultimately in charge.

Ronald Reagan.

Some wonderful news arrived on a perfectly glorious afternoon.

January 20, 1981. Shortly after noon. Reagan stood behind a large wooden podium on the west side of the U.S. Capitol—the austere side, not the one with all the monuments, where many previous presidents had taken the oath of office. His family was right there beside him. Nancy gazed adoringly. Patti was next to her mom. Maureen sat with her new fiancé, Dennis Revell. Ron, who'd recently dropped out of Yale to dance with the Joffrey Ballet, brought his new wife, Doria Palmieri. Michael was there with his wife and son. Loyal and Edith Davis, Nancy's parents, were a row behind them. The VIP section was a sea of familiar faces: Frank Sinatra, Jimmy Stewart, Johnny Carson, William F. Buckley Jr., Henry Kissinger . . . with thousands of other friends, admirers, staffers, political aides, history buffs, tourists, and random Washingtonians stretched out as far as anyone could see.

Just after Reagan recited the oath of office, a screeching squadron of fighter jets burst through the clouds, followed by a twenty-one-gun salute. That's when Richard Allen, the new national security advisor, marched up to the podium and handed the new president a single piece of Situation Room stationery.

Reagan glanced down. "Wheels up in Tehran," the handwritten note said.

After 444 days, Ayatollah Ruhollah Khomeini, the militant Islamic cleric and supreme leader of Iran, had ordered the release of fifty-two American hostages. At that long-awaited moment, the Americans were finally on their way home. Reagan folded the paper and slipped it into his pocket, saying nothing about the note in his 2,452-word inaugural address.

Though the occasion was undeniably formal, Reagan spoke to America and the world in his usual down-to-earth way. "We're too great a nation to limit ourselves to small dreams," he said. "Government isn't the solution to our problem. Government *is* the problem."

Both lines would live for the ages.

It wasn't until Reagan was about to sit for lunch with congressional leaders in the Capitol's Statuary Hall that he broke the news. "With thanks to Almighty God," he said, "I have been given a tagline, the get-off line, that everyone wants for the end of a toast or a speech, or anything else. Some thirty minutes ago, the planes bearing our prisoners left Iranian airspace, and they're now free of Iran."

The hall erupted in wild applause.

At last, the Carter years were over. The Reagan years had begun. All the new president had to do now was govern.

It was a time of high hopes and soaring ambitions, as the start of a new presidential administration almost always is. But hopes and ambitions weren't all it would take for Reagan to govern such a complex nation at such a defining time, even with an enthusiastic cadre of supporters and a landslide victory at the polls. To change America in the ways he had promised to, he and the troika would also need to rethink the role of Big Government, advance his agenda through a sharply divided Congress, and tame the bloated bureaucracy in Washington.

Good luck! That would take more than a day of good news and a few inspiring words.

Much has been written over the years about Reagan's management style. To summarize: He was never much of a detail man. He believed in setting the overall tone and priorities, then counting on his aides, appointees, advisors, and supporters to execute the vision he laid out. Which is a perfectly fine approach . . . if everyone is pulling in the same direction and exhibiting a certain level of competence. But if there's no well-oiled machine to rely on and your own people are constantly crashing into each other and some of them haven't fully signed on to your fundamental aims? Then look out! Trouble ahead!

Unfortunately, the early months of the Reagan administration resembled more of a train wreck than a well-oiled machine.

Crisis after crisis. Blunder after blunder. Too many self-inflicted wounds. The political realities of a self-protective Washington. Constant sniping between the Bush-Ford moderates and the California conservatives. A lack of firm direction from above. A national security apparatus that couldn't seem to make decisions or implement the few that were made. Domestic policy aims that were all over the place. Cabinet members who kept forgetting they were supposed to be part of a team. A president who was slow to drop ineffective people and revisit flawed administrative arrangements early on, even when they caused him repeated embarrassment.

There wasn't one problem. There were many. Yes, the Reagan administration got off to a messy start. And the mismatched troika didn't help. Though the politically moderate Baker was clearly in charge and knew his way around Washington, he was only one of three legs on this wobbly stool. The conservative Meese and Deaver, who had deep, personal ties to Reagan, often sent out messages that conflicted with those of Baker. White House staffers quickly learned that if they didn't get the answer they wanted from one of the three, there were always two other people to ask.

When Jimmy Carter had come into office, he seemed to have a thousand items on his one-hundred-day checklist. While Carter was often accused of micromanaging, everyone in the administration had something to focus on, and they all got busy doing that, often with the president looking over their shoulders and constantly nudging them. If Carter had too many priorities, Reagan may have had too few. He narrowed his focus to four—the economy, national security, the Soviet Union, and streamlining government—and delegated just about everything else. And on even the big four: exactly what to do about them was for others to tease out.

A big part of the problem was the personality profiles of Reagan's cabinet members and agency heads, especially on the foreign policy side. Instead of building a coherent and cooperative team, he chose strong-willed individuals with diverse opinions, all of whom advocated strenuously for their own points of view. Alexander Haig at State, Caspar Weinberger at Defense, Bill Casey at the CIA, Jeane Kirkpatrick at the United Nations: they all had impressive credentials and well-thought-out views. But playing nicely together wasn't what any of them was known for. All of a sudden, they were running off in all different directions, pursuing their own passions, prejudices, and beliefs, which might or might not have reflected the new president's priorities.

The hard-charging Haig began propping up military regimes in Central America, while super spook Casey launched covert operations across the Third World. No one was corralling the administration's foreign policy team to focus on the Soviet Union, Reagan's real priority. One key official who should have been laser focused on that, National Security Advisor Richard Allen, turned out to be a dud. Not only did he quickly get himself in trouble over an unauthorized gratuity from a Japanese media company, he lacked the bureaucratic gravitas or the close Reagan relationship to mediate disputes among the likes of Haig, Weinberger, Casey, and Kirkpatrick or insist that decisions get made. He was soon excluded from cabinet meetings. Confusion and chaos were the inevitable results.

Haig was a special lightning rod, alienating people wherever he went, including the West Wing of the White House. When the secretary tried to make El Salvador a test case for Reagan's anti-communist foreign policy, Congress and the media started howling about human rights. When Haig tried to wrestle China policy away from the White House, making Beijing a strategic ally to block Soviet hegemony, Reagan objected that the policy undermined U.S. loyalty to Taiwan. Then Haig erupted in anger when Reagan skipped over him and appointed Vice President Bush to coordinate White House crisis management. By then, other officials were wondering: Could Haig get along with *anyone*?

Reagan had strong ideas about the Cold War. He believed in winning it! He'd made that plain throughout the campaign. But the administration lacked a coherent policy for containing the Soviet Union, and Reagan was growing impatient about that.

He'd have to find a way to focus the team.

Reagan did get a tremendous outpouring of public support and sympathy two-plus months into the term when a would-be assassin, John Hinckley Jr., shot and wounded him outside the Washington Hilton, also striking press secretary James Brady, Secret Service agent Tim McCarthy, and D.C. police officer Thomas Delahanty. Thankfully, Reagan needed just ten days at George Washington University Hospital. Haig, of course, did what he could to make a tense situation even more so. He promptly declared that with Vice President Bush on a plane, "I am in control here, in the White House." Haig's imagined U.S. Constitution may have dictated such an outcome, but the *real* U.S. Constitution actually had the secretary of state *fifth* in line.

As for Reagan, he took the assassination attempt as he took most things: in stride. When the recuperating president was informed by an aide that he'd be happy to hear that the government was functioning well during his hospitalization, Reagan offered a typically glib response: "What makes you think I'd be happy about that?" When that quote began to circulate, people knew he'd be OK. Asked about the factions that had already grown up inside the administration, the recovering president conceded that internal conflict had indeed become an issue, something he'd been meaning to get around to. "Sometimes, our right hand doesn't know what our far-right hand is doing," he allowed with a familiar shrug.

He didn't miss much. He met with Weinberger and Haig while wearing pajamas in his hospital room, and he was soon back at work full-time in the White House, factions and all.

In the rush to put an economic package together, it didn't take David Stockman, the administration's "boy wonder" management and budget director, any time at all to irritate just about everyone. He upstaged Energy Secretary James Edwards by disclosing an "imminent" order to decontrol oil prices. He got under Haig's skin by proposing sharp cuts in foreign aid. At one early cabinet meeting, Stockman made an instant enemy out of Donald Regan by demanding that the treasury secretary make an on-the-spot decision approving Stockman-favored revisions in the Internal Revenue Code.

And even when everyone on the inside could come together, that was just the start of making policy. It was one thing to talk in the abstract about cutting Big Government. It was quite another, as Reagan quickly discovered, to swing the axe. As the new president's appointees got busy trying to trim the federal bureaucracy, they quickly ran into a reality of American life: every one of those federal programs—Social Security, federal pensions, veterans' benefits, unemployment insurance, welfare payments—was important to *someone* . . . make that *millions of someones*, often as a matter of survival. One national consulting firm totaled it all up: more than 110 million Americans relied directly or indirectly on Washington for at least 25 percent of their income. All those people had congressmen and senators, and they wouldn't sit quietly as benefits were slashed.

It wasn't that Reagan's tax-cutting and fat-trimming goals were impossible, any more than his anti-communist foreign policy goals were. It was just that they would have to be backed by well-coordinated political efforts. It wouldn't be enough to hire a cadre of strong-willed cabinet secretaries and agency chiefs and hope for the best. The same way a coordinated campaign helped to elect Reagan president, so it would take one for him to succeed in the job. Clear messaging. A strategy for taming his opponents. Building public support. But first the people in the new administration had to stop shooting themselves, or each other, in the foot.

Some of the things that happened in those early months were classic rookie mistakes, stumbles that made the new administration look more like the amateur hour. Fights that didn't need to be picked. Tone deafness about how new initiatives were likely to be received. Attorney General William French Smith got slammed for trying to gut the Ethics in Government Act, which called for special prosecutors when high government officials were accused of potential criminality. What was he trying to hide? Bill Brock, the special trade representative, wanted to relax the Foreign Corrupt Practices Act, making it easier for U.S. business executives to bribe foreign officials. Who exactly did he think should be bribed? What message did either of those proposals send? And then there was family. Once his father was in office, Michael Reagan, the president's older son, took a new job selling missile parts to the U.S. government, then reminded federal procurement officials how much

they valued "my father's leadership." Bad look, even if not techni-
cally illegal. Under pressure, young Reagan quit the job.

His father deserved credit for surrounding himself with talented, strong-willed people and giving them the independence to
do their jobs. He just neglected to remind them that they also had
to be part of a team. That message sunk in slowly. It's true that many
first-term administrations have a learning curve to some degree.
But some make very little progress. To Reagan's credit, he learned
as he went along.

The most encouraging sign, a message recognized inside and
out of the White House, was that Reagan pressed gamely along. He
didn't get discouraged. He didn't get mad. He just kept pushing the
things that were important to him and continuing to bond with the
American people who had put him in the job. They'd be his secret
strength going forward.

On April 24, he lifted the Soviet grain embargo to help America's farmers while condemning Soviet occupation of Afghanistan.
On April 28, he appeared in front of a joint session of Congress
and delivered his program for economic recovery. On May 21, he
proposed to Congress a bipartisan effort to fix Social Security. On
June 5, the Centers for Disease Control identified a rare illness that
was primarily afflicting gay men and proposed a plan for fighting it.

Reagan was not advocating for or willing to fight to achieve
small things. His agenda was *big*. It was to take America to the next
level. Best world economy. Biggest job growth in history. Fix enti-
tlement programs. Eliminate communism. Cure disease. Big things
that could make Americans feel good just pursuing them, not to
mention the feeling when those things were achieved.

Those were just some of the steps and the overarching ambitions that would come to define Reagan, Reaganomics, and Reaganism. None of them were instantly successful amid the chaos of those early months and fractured realities of Washington. But Reagan was only getting started, and he was more than happy to learn. He knew how to lead. He knew how to bring people together. He knew how to win. A killer combination.

CHAPTER 9

BREAKING BARRIERS

When Reagan said he'd put a woman on the U.S. Supreme Court, when he vowed to tame Big Government, Big Business, and Big Labor, a lot of people thought those were just words. What those people failed to understand was that Reagan actually meant them.

LESSON LEARNED:
DON'T JUST SAY WHAT YOU MEAN. . . . DO IT.

There was some wiggle room in the campaign promise . . . and some lingering questions about why Ronald Reagan had decided to make it.

If elected president, he announced two weeks before Election Day, he'd name a woman to "one of the first Supreme Court vacancies in my administration."

One of the first . . .

"It is time for a woman to sit among our highest jurists," Reagan emphasized that day in California. "I will also seek out women to appoint to other federal courts in an effort to bring about a better balance on the federal bench."

What motivated that pledge remains a topic of debate all these years later. Reagan had always been leery of quotas, affirmative action, or anything else that relied on race, gender, or other such categories to fill job openings—in government or the private sector. In his eight years as governor of California, he'd made three appointments to the state Supreme Court. All three went to men.

Did Reagan have a philosophical epiphany that October? Or did politics persuade him to do something he wouldn't normally have done? In the final lap of the 1980 campaign, his appearances were being picketed over his opposition to the Equal Rights Amendment. And the polls consistently showed him running weaker with women than with men. The same day he said "it's time" for more women on the federal bench, a *New York Times* poll showed him beating Jimmy Carter by a solid 11 points in Illinois but still trailing by 9 points with the state's female voters.

There had to be a reason for that.

Asked about his persistent gender gap, Reagan said he thought it had more to do with war and peace than with equal rights, the scary image of the Hollywood cowboy with his finger on the nuclear button. "I would think it might reflect some success with the false charges made by the president and others that I might be prone to turn to war. I think women might be more affected by that." But whatever the reason, candidate Reagan clearly had some ground to make up with women, and he landed on the potent symbol of the all-male U.S. Supreme Court. In the court's 191-year history, not a single woman had ever been nominated, much less fitted for a dowdy black robe.

If he was really prepared to change that, President Reagan didn't have to wait long.

Justice Potter Stewart was an Eisenhower appointee still best remembered for "I know it when I see it," his hard-to-argue-with definition of obscenity (*Jacobellis v. Ohio*, 1964). On June 18, 1981, not quite five months after Reagan moved into the White House, Stewart announced his retirement from the court after twenty-three years. Now the rookie president had a decision to make, one of the most consequential of his entire time in office, since vacancies on the nation's top court are so rare and the justices can serve for life.

So, what would the president do? Would he fall back on a technicality and try to climb out of his words from the campaign trail?

No, actually.

A promise was a promise, Reagan decided, even a promise that had been made with some wiggle room. Sure, he could have nominated a man and still said "one" of his Supreme Court appointments would go to a woman, assuming he got more than one. But Reagan didn't play that game.

How strongly did he feel about his campaign promise? Very, even before he had a vacancy to fill. In his first month as president, he had directed his top advisors to put together a list of the very best potential Supreme Court prospects, asking them to focus on "constitutionally oriented" women. He wanted to be ready if and when a seat opened up.

The list he got back had eight names, including four women.

He told the advisors to narrow the choices for him. When the short list arrived, two women were included, Sandra Day O'Connor, a state appellate judge from Arizona, and Amalya Kearse, who'd been appointed by Jimmy Carter to the Second Circuit Court of Appeals in New York. If Kearse was nominated and the Senate confirmed, she wouldn't only be the first woman on the nation's top court. She'd also be the first African American woman.

Reagan's troika still had doubts. They said they weren't convinced that a woman was necessarily the right way to go. They added the names of two "more conservative jurists" to the list, Antonin Scalia and Robert Bork, reminding Reagan that any appointment he got might easily be his last. Shouldn't he choose someone as conservative as he was?

No sale.

On July 6, three weeks after Justice Stewart's announcement, Reagan was on the phone to Arizona. "Called Judge O'Connor and told her she was my nominee for Supreme Court," he wrote in his diary that day. "Already the flak is starting and from my own supporters. Right to Life people say she is pro-abortion. She declares abortion is personally repugnant to her. I think she'll make a good justice."

O'Connor's personal story was powerfully inspiring, indicative of the era . . . and very Old West. Born in El Paso, Texas, she'd grown up on a 198,000-acre cattle ranch near Duncan, Arizona. Her family had no indoor plumbing. They were nine miles from the nearest paved road. She'd been shooting jackrabbits and coyotes since she had pigtails. When she graduated from Stanford Law School, the future judge couldn't find a paying job because of her gender. Her plan B: volunteering—no salary and no office—as a legal researcher in the San Mateo County district attorney's office. After marrying and raising three children in the Phoenix area, she worked in Barry Goldwater's 1964 presidential campaign, served as an assistant Arizona attorney general, got elected to the Arizona senate, and rose to majority leader before becoming a judge—in the Maricopa County Superior Court and then on the state Court of Appeals.

Every time O'Connor encountered a glass ceiling, she busted right through it. If that wasn't an inspiring, Reagan-style anecdote, nothing was.

Reagan was right about that flak from the right. Though some conservatives held their fire because they liked so much else about Reagan, many complained that the judge's views on abortion seemed squishy. They weren't entirely wrong about that. Her record did show she had equivocal feelings about outlawing abortion in Arizona after 1973's *Roe v. Wade*. She wasn't the real hard-liner some of the right were hoping for, that was for sure.

In fulfilling one promise, was Reagan breaking another one: to appoint staunchly pro-life judges? That's what some of the critics charged, picking up on the objections that the troika raised. "We're made to look like fools," grumbled Peter Gemma, executive director of the National Pro-Life Political Action Committee. "Reagan bends over backwards to please those who have something against him."

The Religious Right was already up in arms. "All good Christians should be concerned about the O'Connor appointment," said the Moral Majority's Jerry Falwell, to which Barry Goldwater,

O'Connor's senator and former political mentor, immediately shot back: "I think every good Christian ought to kick Falwell right in the ass."

Republican senators Steve Symms, Jesse Helms, and Don Nickles all called the White House to complain. "Pro-family Republican senators will not support O'Connor," Nickles warned. But the opposition turned out to be hollower than it seemed. O'Connor made a good impression in her confirmation hearing before the Senate Judiciary Committee. Reagan hung tough. In the end, all three of the nay-saying senators voted to confirm her, as did every other voting member of the U.S. Senate, Republicans and Democrats. The tally on September 21 was 99–0. Only Senator Max Baucus of Montana was absent, and he sent O'Connor a copy of *A River Runs Through It* and an apology note.

Imagine this: keeping a promise to the voters, appointing a woman to the Supreme Court, standing up to the opposition from both parties, and nominating an immensely qualified jurist can lead to a unanimous vote in the U.S. Senate. Wow! Those were the good old days! The question for today is: Can that kind of leadership produce a similar result? Can *any* kind?

As for Reagan, he looked reasonable compared to some of the people who'd been slamming his nominee. Whatever turmoil was still stirring in his administration—and, clearly, there was some—none of it sidetracked the court choice. Coming out on top, Reagan knew, was often a matter of how well you picked your opponents . . . or how lucky you were when they picked you. He'd done well this time. In stark contrast to Gemma, Falwell, Symms, Helms, and

Nickles, Reagan made history by nominating a judge he genuinely admired, who also happened to be a woman.

Key to Reagan's appeal—and an important part of his strong connection with regular Americans—was his insistent plainspokenness.

Yes, he was an experienced actor, comfortable delivering other people's words. Yes, he'd been a professional broadcaster, public speaker, and advertising pitchman, fields renowned for their carefully crafted messaging. But Reagan had his own strong feelings about the best way to communicate, and that was clearly and directly, without a lot of flourish or sophistication.

He liked anecdotes, individual, human stories to illustrate larger arguments, like O'Connor's. He was constantly dropping those. But he always got around to making his points as plainly as he could, whatever his aides and advisors might have been whispering in the background. He knew what he believed, and he didn't mind saying so. *Government's too large. . . . Taxes are too high. . . . The Soviet Union is our enemy. . . . Wars have to be won. . . .* He was not a fancy talker, on or off the campaign trail.

Partly, this came from his Midwestern upbringing, where accusing someone of "being slick" or "putting on airs" were two of the worst insults you could hurl. Part of it was his well-earned disgust for politics as usual, on both sides of the aisle: fast-talking candidates who promised all sorts of things, most of which were quickly forgotten after Election Day. People were sick of that, Reagan thought. He knew he was. So despite a well-earned reputation for eloquence, his version of eloquence was always planted firmly on the ground. Its literary ancestors were Mark Twain, Jack London, and Ernest Hemingway, not William Faulkner or even William Shakespeare. While preparing his inaugural address, Reagan had instructed his speechwriters to tone *down* the language of an early draft, making it less soaring, less grandly poetic, more down-to-earth and conversational. He didn't want to preach to the people. He wanted to talk to them. He wasn't shooting for the stars like John F. Kennedy. His aim was much closer to home.

So it was with the promises that he made on his way to the presidency.

When he said "it is time" for a woman to join the Supreme Court, he meant it was time. When he referred to "one of the first Supreme Court vacancies in my administration," that might have given him a chance to bob and weave if he'd wanted to. But he didn't. He'd heard about a woman in Arizona with a stirring personal narrative and a long list of accomplishments in politics and the law, and he went with her. She was a lifelong Republican of high character, mature temperament, and generally conservative views. She'd even grown up on a ranch.

And if Jerry Falwell didn't like it—well, what was it that Barry Goldwater had said?

Reagan had no particular beef with Professional Air Traffic Controllers Organization, the union representing the people at major U.S. airports who guided the planes safely on and off the ground.

Lots of federal agencies had unionized workforces. PATCO

hadn't been especially militant over the years. The union even endorsed Reagan against Jimmy Carter in the 1980 campaign. And why not? The controllers hardly fit the old stereotype of overpaid, underworked government employees. The typical federal air traffic controller (a GS-13) earned $36,613 a year, nearly 20 percent less than their private-sector counterparts. Many of them were military veterans, working-class guys without college degrees who'd built suburban lives for themselves and their families with skills they'd learned in the service. These were Ronald Reagan's people. And you couldn't say the job wasn't important or that any idiot could do it.

But when contract negotiations heated up in February 1981, things quickly turned sour between the union and the Federal Aviation Administration. Though the workers demanded a hefty raise, money wasn't the main sticking point. It was benefits and working conditions, including a better retirement plan and a thirty-two-hour, four-day workweek, which the union negotiators characterized as a safety issue. "You don't want exhausted controllers nodding off during their shifts!" the union negotiators warned, more than a little threateningly. Fair enough. You definitely wouldn't want that. But the talks stalled there . . . and stayed stalled.

For months.

At which point PATCO president Robert Poli badly misjudged Ronald Reagan. The union declared a strike at 7:00 a.m. on August 3, assuming that the president would immediately pressure the FAA into accepting most of PATCO's demands. The union had endorsed him, hadn't they? That kind of thinking was plainly unwise. No one should have doubted the Republican president's resolve. Just one day earlier, the White House had warned the air traffic controllers in no uncertain terms: There'd be "no amnesty" for strikers. And there'd be no negotiations during an illegal strike.

The mass walkout was a clear violation of federal law, which prohibited strikes by federal government employees. Though he wasn't initially gunning for PATCO, Reagan declared the strike a "peril to national safety." Citing the 1947 Taft-Hartley Act, he ordered the workers back to their control towers and their computer monitors. Of the nearly 13,000 controllers, only 1,300 returned.

It was a real showdown. At that point Reagan had three choices. He could give the controllers what they were asking for. He could shut down the U.S. air travel system indefinitely. Or he could fire the workers and go about the business of hiring replacements. The first-year president didn't hesitate. He went with option number three.

This, too, was an example of Ronald Reagan living up to his promises and his core beliefs, even if it meant veering from the easier political path. All throughout the campaign, he had included Big Labor—along with Big Government and Big Business—as one of the runaway forces he vowed to rein in. He was especially suspicious of public employee unions. Police officers. Firefighters. Schoolteachers. Public health and welfare workers. Though they had the legal right to unionize, these public servants were supposed to be servants of the people. The people were counting on them. The nation simply couldn't function if these vital workers abandoned their posts every time they wanted a raise. That certainly applied to air traffic controllers. What was next? Would U.S. Army privates start signing pledge cards to establish a soldiers' union?

There had to be limits to the tactics that public employee unions used in their negotiations, he said. In Reagan's view, the air traffic controllers had just crossed that line.

Just before 11:00 a.m. on August 3, four hours after the workers abandoned their posts, he stood in the White House Rose Garden and spoke to the controllers and the nation. He'd prepared the statement himself. It was written in longhand, and he hadn't let any of his anxious advisors change a word.

This was not an inevitable strike, he said. "This was the culmination of seven months of negotiations between the Federal Aviation Administration and the union.

"At one point in these negotiations, agreement was reached and signed by both sides granting a $40 million increase in salaries and benefits." But that deal fell apart, and the demands the workers were making now "would impose a tax burden on their fellow citizens which is unacceptable."

Unlike some Republican leaders, Reagan emphasized, he was not anti-union. He was a lifelong member of the AFL-CIO and the first president in American history ever to have *union president* on his résumé. "I respect the right of workers in the private sector to strike," he said. But "Government cannot close down the assembly line. It has to provide without interruption the protective services which are Government's reason for being."

The controllers knew the law, he said. "Let me read the solemn oath taken by each of these employees, a sworn affidavit, when they accepted their jobs: 'I am not participating in any strike against the Government of the United States or any agency thereof . . .'"

How much clearer could that be?

"It is for this reason that I must tell those who fail to report for duty this morning they are in violation of the law, and if they do not report for work within forty-eight hours they have forfeited their jobs and will be terminated."

That's what he said, and that's what happened. The vast majority of the nation's air traffic controllers became *former* air traffic controllers, 11,345 in all, while their bosses at the FAA manned the control towers and scrambled to interview and hire replacements.

No one was more surprised than union president Poli. "We could be accused of miscalculation," he was forced to admit that week. "I was surprised . . . I didn't really believe that they would have taken such harsh actions." No one could remember the last time a president had fired an entire federal workforce like that. But Reagan felt like he had no choice. He could let the nation's air travel system be held hostage. But he'd seen what happened in Iran when an American president felt paralyzed by hostage takers. Reagan wasn't going to make the same mistake at home. And if other unionized federal employees got the message from this debacle— don't even *think* of striking!—well, so much the better.

The strike was painful for almost everyone: the airlines, their customers, the relative handful of controllers who returned to work, and certainly for the many thousands who found themselves suddenly out on the street. The nation's air traffic control system groaned ahead, however. Five years in, some of the striking controllers would be rehired, but only a few hundred of them. Together, the replacement workers and those who returned would start a new union, the National Air Traffic Controllers Association.

That organization advocated for better wages, benefits, and working conditions, like all unions do. But somewhere in there,

WHAT WOULD REAGAN DO?

they seemed to have learned a lesson. They didn't even hint of going out on strike.

Over the next seven-plus years of his presidency, Reagan would have plenty of other opportunities to put his words into action, speaking directly to the American people about himself, his policies, and his personal inclinations. About his age and work habits: "I have left orders to be awakened at any time in case of national emergency, even if I'm in a cabinet meeting." About his testy relations with the media: "Before I refuse to take your questions, I have an opening statement." About his time in Hollywood: "How can a president *not* be an actor?" Reaching all the way back to his own father's appreciation for the absurdities of life, heavy dollops of humor were in the mix.

It was easy to dismiss comments like those as passing, light-hearted quips. In fact, there were serious messages inside all of them. *I'm still with it, despite what my enemies are saying. . . . I'm not intimidated by the media. . . . I'm not ashamed of who I am. . . .* Truly, only someone with genuine self-confidence could joke like that about his own alleged foibles. Whatever else might be said about Reagan, he never lacked self-confidence. This was obvious in how he communicated on issues large and small.

Consequently, Democratic congressional leaders and America's staunchest enemies abroad rarely had any doubt about how the president felt. About the future of Eastern Europe: "Mr. Gorbachev, tear down this wall!" About fiscal responsibility: "Balancing the budget is a little like protecting your virtue: you just have to learn to say no." About the absurd bigness of Big Government: "Government's view of the economy could be summed up in a few short phrases: If it moves, tax it. If it keeps moving, regulate it. And if it stops moving, subsidize it."

Any confusion? I didn't think so!

And good luck trying to answer any of those arguments with white papers, data points, or a chart and an easel. Reagan spoke a more powerful language: from his heart.

You might not like what he was saying. You might not agree with his views. You might not even find the quips funny, though most of them *were* pretty funny. But chances are when he said he was going to do something, he would.

There are endless examples, but none of them set the tone of his eight-year presidency like the nomination of Sandra Day O'Connor and the firing of the air traffic controllers. That's where Reagan put everyone on notice. Now that he was in the White House, he'd be the same straight talker he'd been on the lecture circuit and on the campaign trail. If you wanted to know what he was thinking or what his next move would be, all you had to do was listen to him.

That clarity of thought and motive is wholly lacking in much of today's American politics. Recriminations. Threats. Drama. Name-calling. Subpoenas. Social media insults. They have raised the national temperature and lowered the national character—and lowered our standing in the world. Reagan would understand: on that trade-off, the juice is truly not worth the squeeze. The anxiety and anger of America isn't inevitable. It can be salved by Reagan-esque clarity and leadership.

CHAPTER 10

BEST BUDS

Reagan had an extraordinary gift for making people like him, even lifelong Democratic pols. He learned to use that charm to achieve major things for America. But at his core, Reagan was still something of a loner, and that could be difficult for those who were closest to him.

LESSON LEARNED: IT'S HARDER TO HATE UP CLOSE.

"Did you hear the one about Mrs. Flanagan?"

It was an off-color joke between a couple of Irish American guys of a certain age, one nearing seventy, the other just past it. That's what broke the ice that day for Tip O'Neill and Ronald Reagan. And Reagan was the one who delivered the folksy setup and the potty-mouthed punchline.

If you don't like off-color humor, you should probably skip the next few paragraphs. Otherwise, here's the Gaelic ditty that Reagan shared: One day Mrs. Flanagan was feeling sickly and went to the doctor for a look-at. The doctor checked her out and said, "Well now, Mrs. Flanagan, I'm perplexed at your condition. But if you bring a urine specimen to me in the morning, I can tell exactly what's wrong."

Mrs. Flanagan went home and said to her husband, "What's a urine specimen?"

"I don't know," Mr. Flanagan replied, shaking his head. "But if you go see Mrs. O'Toole, she'll know what to do."

Mrs. Flanagan went down the road to Mrs. O'Toole's and returned a few minutes later with her clothes torn, a black eye, bruises all over her body, and her hair tangled like a bird's nest. "Jesus, Mary, and Joseph!" her shocked husband gasped. "What happened to ye?"

"I went to see Mrs. O'Toole and asked her what a urine specimen is, and she said, 'Piss in a bottle, woman.' So I said, 'Go shit in yer hat!' and the fight was on."

O-K!

That may not be everyone's idea of high comedy. But given the ages and backgrounds of the Democratic Speaker of the House of Representatives and the Republican president of the United States, they were definitely talking each other's language. So the bonding was on . . . just when they needed it most.

This was April 28, 1982, about one-third of the way through Reagan's first term in the White House. From day one, as he pressed his conservative agenda of business deregulation, tax cuts, and higher military spending, he'd been getting stubborn resistance from O'Neill, who didn't like the sound of any of that and feared the new president was coming next for Social Security and Medicare. But now the two pols needed each other. The budget deficit was rising rapidly—too rapidly even for some Democrats. The stock market had peaked after the election and been dropping like a stone ever since. The credit-rating agencies were grumbling loudly. Whatever their disagreements, neither side wanted to wreck the U.S. economy. What the moment demanded, Reagan decided, was the application of some lighthearted Irish charm and a friendly sit-down with the Democratic boss of the House. So he climbed into the Beast, the presidential limo, and took a sixteen-block ride from the White House to Capitol Hill, where he paid a call on the Speaker.

Reagan was well aware of all that divided the two men, the liberal Democrat from Massachusetts and the conservative Republican from California via Iowa and Illinois. But Reagan had always trusted his ability to connect with another human being and reach some kind of mutual understanding, even with someone vastly different from himself. If he could get inside another person's head, he knew great things could happen. Isn't that what acting is? Connecting with the members of the audience, then taking them somewhere they didn't expect to go? It was all a matter of tapping into a shared humanity. Never forgetting who you are and what you are hoping to achieve . . . while finding a place where the wants and the needs of both sides overlap. And it was built—in Reagan's case, at least—on what the Irish liked to call the "gift of gab." Anyone could see that Reagan and O'Neill both had heavy blessings of it. Both men had started out in extremely modest circumstances. That gift had already taken them far in life. And one of the best ways to get the ball rolling, Reagan understood, was to sit down together and put a smile on the other fellow's face. It's a whole lot easier to hate someone at a distance than to loathe the person who's sitting next to you, especially if he's just made you laugh.

Paging Mrs. Flanagan!

They met in the President's Room, just off the Senate floor, where Lyndon Johnson had signed the 1965 Voting Rights Act and where, immediately after the inauguration, Reagan had signed his first round of cabinet nominations and an order freezing federal employment. But this was not another official event. It was more of a cozy chitchat. After the ribald yucks, the two men expressed their mutual desire to keep the economy on track—how important that was to American business and to the millions and millions of people who counted on steady, decent-paying jobs. Republican tax cuts had their place, O'Neill allowed. But he also made the Democratic point that government needed revenue to fund programs both sides considered vital. The two men agreed they would work together to come up with some kind of plan.

It took a few months of back-and-forth as their aides sorted out the particulars. But the first result of that effort was the Tax Equity and Fiscal Responsibility Act of 1982, which reduced the federal budget gap by cutting spending, closing tax loopholes, tightening up enforcement, and taking other steps. Reagan signed the bill the Friday before Labor Day. And with confidence gained from that experience, they kept moving forward. In January, with O'Neill's support, President Reagan raised the gas tax for the first time in twenty-three years. He didn't like doing it, but it was time, he decided. Fiscal responsibility wasn't always *fun*. Working together, Reagan and O'Neill also established the bipartisan National Commission on Social Security Reform, and both men eventually endorsed a package of changes that included raising the retirement age and delaying a cost-of-living increase. To the surprise of some Republicans, O'Neill agreed to all of that. And it just might have saved Social Security.

Would the president and the Speaker's knack for finding common ground turn these two staunch rivals into committed allies? Would they abandon their lifelong political proclivities to sing in middle-of-the-road harmony! No way! Not a chance! They'd keep pushing and pulling at each other until the day Reagan left Washington—and they wouldn't stop taking their shots even then. But after the Capitol sit-down, working together for the good of America was at least a possibility, one of the tricks that both men now had up their sleeves.

This wasn't a new realization on either man's part. The political reality was plain from the day Reagan arrived in Washington: Republicans had a solid majority in the U.S. Senate. So the new president could pretty much count on the Senate. Pretty much. Tennessee's Howard Baker, the Senate majority leader, had a far more Washington-centric view of the world than Reagan did. But he was a Capitol Hill insider who knew how to get things done. He'd be an ally. Still, the Democrats were in firm control of the House of Representatives with a 51-vote margin, 243 to 192. To make any progress there, Reagan had to deal with the Democratic Speaker, who controlled the House calendar, not to mention a solid majority of the votes.

CHRIS CHRISTIE

Still, Reagan's charm offensive had gotten off to a rocky start, fourteen months before political reality (and Mrs. Flanagan) saved him. A month after the inauguration, he and Nancy invited Tip and Mildred O'Neill and a small group of others for dinner in the White House family quarters, which Nancy had been busily freshening up. By all accounts, it was a pleasant evening. Before calling it a night, the Speaker even complimented the First Lady on her renovations: "You know, I've been in and out of this place for twenty-seven years, and I have never seen it look as beautiful as this."

A bit of Irish blarney? Perhaps. Still, that first attempt at friend winning didn't have quite the impact the new president had hoped it would. A couple of days later, as Reagan recalled in his memoir, "I picked up a newspaper and read a story in which Tip really lit into me personally because he didn't like the economic recovery program and some of the cuts proposed in spending. Some of his remarks were pretty nasty. I wasn't only surprised but disappointed and also a little hurt."

He called the Speaker the next morning. "Tip," he said, "I just read in the paper what you said about me yesterday. I thought we had a pretty fine relationship going."

"Ol' buddy," Tip said, "that's politics. After six o'clock we can be friends. But before six, it's politics."

The Speaker had decades of experience in the trenches of Washington. For Reagan, this was fresh terrain. Suddenly, Jesse Unruh and the Hollywood studio bosses seemed like pussycats compared to these Washington players. They needed to be worked. Reagan understood that, and he was committed to doing what it took to succeed, a message he made sure his staff was also committed to.

When Reagan was shot on March 30, 1981, White House chief of staff James Baker made sure that Tip O'Neill was the first politician granted access to the hospital room. No one had to explain to Tip what that meant or how he should behave. The Speaker came up to the room, knelt at the president's bedside, and recited the Twenty-Third Psalm:

> *The Lord is my shepherd, I shall not want . . . Even though I walk through the valley of the shadow of death, I fear no evil, for thou art with me . . .*

And even that wasn't enough. It would still take another year and that sit-down at the Capitol for the parameters of their personal connection to be clear to both men. These things don't happen overnight. But both of them realized the importance of a productive working relationship, and they eventually got there. That relationship would become one of the defining realities of Reagan's presidency—so real that O'Neill could say something like this, with Reagan sitting right beside him, at a St. Patrick's Day (!) banquet in 1986:

"The president and I oftentimes don't see eye to eye. We have our little squabbles. But when he calls me at night and he says, 'Is it six o'clock? Can we talk friendly?' 'Sure. Absolutely.' So we swap an Irish story or two. Mr. President, you know we have different philosophies. But I want to tell you how much I admire your ability, your talent, the way you handle the American people, the love that the American people have for you and your leadership, even though I have opposed it."

Talk about another era! It's almost impossible to imagine one of our recent House Speakers talking like that about a president from the other party. Remarkable! And it kept producing big, tangible results.

Instructive though it is, there is more to the story than this. Like most fascinating people, Ronald Reagan was a man of layers. He was more than one thing. He had public and private sides, and they weren't always the same. Yes, he could bond easily with strangers, charm Tip O'Neill, and get a crowd to stand and cheer. But he could also be distant and reserved, even a bit chilly, to the people who were closest to him.

Especially to the people who were closest to him.

It's one of the real paradoxes of Ronald Reagan.

It would be a mistake to portray Reagan as hail-fellow-well-met and then leave it at that. To understand the man is also to recognize his complexities.

White House speechwriter Peggy Noonan, who helped to craft some of her boss's most memorable phrases, called this other side of Reagan his "famous detachment." Wrote Noonan: "We have all noticed in life that big people with big virtues not infrequently have big flaws, too." In Noonan's up-close view, Reagan's big flaw resided in his personality, as distinct from his character: "his famous detachment, which was painful for his children and disorienting for his staff."

Noonan wasn't the only White House staffer to notice this—or to take it personally. James Baker, Donald Regan, Larry Speakes,

Martin Anderson, and many other close aides have remarked at one time or another that they felt a frozen distance between themselves and the president they loved and admired, no matter how long or how closely they worked with him. Despite his general cheerfulness, they all seem to agree: he just didn't seem that interested in them. Or maybe he was too busy with other things.

"No one around him quite understood it, the deep and emotional engagement in public events and public affairs, and the slight and seemingly formal interest in the lives of those around him," wrote Noonan.

It's not that Reagan was grumpy or rude or short with anyone, his close aides say. It's more that he had his own ways of doing things and didn't care to change . . . for anyone.

"He had this appearance of being friendly and jovial and nice, never argued with anyone, never complained," marveled Anderson, a renowned economist who'd worked in the Nixon White House and then helped Reagan flesh out the original program that became known as Reaganomics. "But if you shook your head and thought about it a little bit, he always did it his way. It was like there was a steel bar right down the middle of him and everything you touched was soft and fuzzy except the steel bar in the middle. He always did it his way. No matter how many people talked to him, no matter what happened, he always did it his way. If you were in the way, you were gone, you were fired. He never took any pleasure out of it, just gone." The staffers who lasted were the ones who understood that.

Anderson had a memorable phrase for this aspect of the president's personality. Reagan, he said, was a "warmly ruthless man."

Those who worked in the White House debated what might

explain this gulf between the public Reagan and the private Reagan, the gregarious, charming, expansive leader and the far more confined man. Did he just not notice those immediately around him? Was he so focused on his larger goals that he had no emotional room for casual give-and-take? Which was *the real Reagan?* Well, both were, of course. They were two different layers of the same complex man.

Whether it was a conscious strategy or just a deeply ingrained character trait, his aides were never quite sure. But no one could deny it worked for him. "To be respected, even loved, by one's subordinates, while remaining distant from them can be useful to a president," argued Everett Carll Ladd, a savvy pollster at the University of Connecticut who studied Reagan closely. "The distance strengthens his authority. Avoiding emotional engagement is functional: Much more important matters should claim a president's psychic energy."

That personal distance, I believe, was part of what gave Reagan the capacity to persevere even in the face of strenuous opposition. See the Democrats in Congress. See the protracted battles over tax policy, military spending, and budget cuts. See the constant barrage of media attacks portraying Reagan as an airheaded movie star, a right-wing ideologue, a flat-out racist, and, as time went on, a senile coot who was supposedly losing touch with reality. He bore all those insults and more. Yet he never seemed to let any of them get under his skin. There was a protective shell around him. Instead of erupting in anger, he reacted with a smile and a shrug. Reagan knew who he was and what he believed in, and no one was going to convince him otherwise. Hard as it might sometimes be on those around him, his man-alone outlook ensured that nothing would stand in his way or slow him down.

But as Ladd added somewhat ominously with Reagan clearly in mind: "What works well politically may not seem benign in familial relationships." It was a point Peggy Noonan also made.

Among those who struggled with this were Reagan's four children, Maureen, Michael, Patti, and Ron. In their books and in various interviews, they all recall him as a good dad, a kind dad, a supportive dad—but not an especially warm one. There's a reason that Michael Reagan, the president's older, adopted son, decided to call his autobiography *On the Outside Looking In*.

"My childhood," Michael writes, "was spent seeking affection, trying to get my parents to put their arms around me and say, 'I love you.'" Michael's mother, Jane Wyman, comes in for the harshest criticism. But his father also comes off as decidedly formal and distant across the decades. The exuberant, magnetic, open-hearted pied piper who made so many people love Reagan when he was out in the world? Remember that guy? The one who connected so deftly with Tip O'Neill? There wasn't much sign of him at home. Right before the second inauguration, the thirty-nine-year-old Michael grabbed a rare moment alone with his dad and confronted him: "You know, you've never told me that you love me."

His father "looked surprised," Michael writes. "Then he said, 'Michael, I love you.'"

And that was pretty much that.

Reagan's older son describes his relationship with his father in the same way the White House aides describe theirs: as civil and decent and rarely critical but still not close. In Michael Reagan's view and others', too, the only exceptions to this general rule were the two strongest women in Ronald Reagan's life.

His mother, Nelle, and his wife Nancy.

Anyone who spent five minutes exploring Reagan's childhood can't help but notice how crucial his mother was in focusing him, directing him, and making him feel secure. Decades later, the same was true of Nancy. No one was closer to him than she was. No one understood him like she did.

Nancy had clearly thought about all this a lot. She didn't address it directly while her husband was in the White House, but she shared her insights in 1989. At heart, she said, her husband was a loner.

"He doesn't let anybody get too close. There's a wall around him."

She traced this back to the constant upheavals of his hard-scrabble childhood as the Reagans moved from house to house and town to town. "It's hard to make close friends or to put down roots when you're always moving, and I think this—plus the fact that everybody knew his father was an alcoholic—explained why Ronnie became a loner. Although he loves people, he often seems remote, and he doesn't let anybody get too close."

Even she could sometimes feel that distance, she said. "There's a wall around him. He lets me come closer than anyone else, but there are times when even I feel that barrier." Compared to most people, she said, her husband was remarkably self-contained. "Ronnie is an affable and gregarious man who enjoys other people, but unlike most of us he doesn't need them for companionship or approval. As he himself has told me, he seems to need only one other person—me."

CHAPTER 11

FOUR MORE

As he sought reelection, Reagan's record of achievement was impressive. His poll numbers were strong. But one issue lurked just below the surface, sure to explode before Election Day. At seventy-three, was he *too old* to be president for another four years? Of course, Reagan had an answer for that.

LESSON LEARNED:
YOU'RE ONLY AS *BOLD* AS YOU FEEL.

It wasn't much fun being a Democrat during the Reagan years, especially not a liberal Democrat. Charming as Reagan could be, most people in politics don't enjoy losing, and the Dems had to endure quite a bit of that.

They got an early view of their future when Reagan's coattails helped to flip the Senate to a Republican majority after the 1980 election, costing the other party eleven seats. Republicans gained another two Senate seats two years later in the midterms. Though Democrats retained their solid majority in the House of Representatives, Reagan's leadership and negotiating skills produced a killer record for the president to run on in 1984.

Lowering taxes. Slashing government regulations. Turning the economy around. Strengthening the military. Staring down the air traffic controllers. Putting the first woman on the U.S. Supreme Court. And for an extra dash of feel-good drama, rescuing six hundred American medical students from the island nation of Grenada while deposing a communist regime that had seized power in a violent coup. That was the first major overseas action by U.S. troops since the end of the Vietnam War, and it was over in less than a week.

Democratic leaders in Washington had objections to plenty of that. But here was the really maddening part as far as they were concerned: a lot of rank-and-file Democrats liked it all just fine. And they liked the Republican president who was getting all those things done. Reagan had been so successful in nailing down the support of moderate Democrats in northern states, a whole new voter identity category was now enshrined in the lexicon of American politics: *Reagan Democrats*. It turned out these Reagan Democrats were popping up pretty much everywhere, including some places you might not expect to find them. In cities and suburbs on the East and West Coasts. Across the industrial Midwest. My home state of New Jersey was positively crawling with them, especially in counties like Middlesex and Gloucester, which were solidly Democratic but which I'd win in both my races for governor. Men and women who'd identified as Democrats all their lives. They'd come from Democratic families. Maybe they belonged to a Democratic-leaning union. But in Ronald Reagan they found a

Republican leader who spoke *to* and *for* them while the Democratic Party had been lurching leftward since the rise of New Left figures like Eugene McCarthy and George McGovern. Many of these Reagan Democrats repeated a phrase that Reagan had used after he switched parties in 1962: "I didn't leave the Democratic Party. The Democratic Party left me." These Reagan Democrats weren't hard-core conservatives. Many of them still thought of themselves as commonsense Democrats. They simply felt more comfortable with Reagan's pro-military, pro-work, pro-family outlook, and they didn't like what their own party was offering them. Plus, they liked Reagan the man—just *liked* him—which is a far more powerful force in politics than many Washington insiders tend to recognize.

Reagan had the Republican Party unified behind him. He didn't have to worry about a primary challenger. But if he wanted four more years, he'd still have to win reelection in November of 1984, and the Democrats certainly weren't going to just concede the race. They'd had plenty of time to plan their anti-Reagan counteroffensive as they stewed through all those frustrating defeats at the hands of the popular Republican president. Would the Democrats craft a platform that at least *sounded* good? Perhaps. Would they portray Reagan as an extremist, a bigot, an aging has-been or a world-stage cowboy? They'd certainly try. Would they find a Democratic nominee who would excite their base, attract the middle, and bring the Reagan Democrats back home? That remained to be seen.

Reagan and his political team felt confident as the election year began. But until the Democrats chose a nominee and the American people began to respond, no one really knew what to expect. Everyone remembered what happened the last time. Reagan beat Jimmy

Carter in a national landslide, grabbing the highest number of electoral votes ever won by a nonincumbent presidential candidate. But that was against Jimmy Carter. The Democrats might choose a stronger nominee this time, someone who could appeal to moderates as well as the party's liberal side, maybe even remind those Reagan Democrats where they came from. That would have been the smart strategy, reversing some of the excesses that had weakened their party, enlarging instead of shrinking the Democratic tent. But the internal politics of the Democratic Party wouldn't allow it.

Sure, a few moderate Democrats entered the primary campaign. Ohio senator and former astronaut John Glenn. Former Florida governor Reubin Askew. Senator Fritz Hollings of South Carolina. But those three were out of it by March, and the three leading Democrats all came from the party's liberal wing. Walter Mondale, who'd been Carter's vice president, was an old-line Great Society liberal in the mold of fellow Minnesotan Hubert Humphrey. Senator Gary Hart of Colorado, the "New Ideas" candidate, had managed George McGovern's disastrous 1972 campaign, losing forty-nine states that year. Reverend Jesse Jackson positioned himself even further to the left as the voice of the disenfranchised and only the second African American to run a national campaign for president (after Shirley Chisholm). It was hard to imagine how any of these three would bring the Reagan Democrats home.

Each of them appealed to a different slice of the left: Mondale had the older crowd. Hart spoke more to younger voters. Jackson focused his message on minorities and the poor. If there was one key moment, it came during a televised debate in March when Mondale dismissed Hart's "New Ideas" platform as shallow and lacking in specifics. Mondale said his opponent's rhetoric reminded him of the Wendy's commercial that was all over TV that fall:

"Where's the beef?"

The audience howled, Hart looked shaken, and Mondale went on to accept the Democratic nomination at the Moscone Center in San Francisco the third week of July, naming New York congresswoman Geraldine Ferraro as his running mate and setting the stage for a Reagan-Mondale showdown in November.

Reagan's political team wanted their candidate to avoid specifics in the reelection campaign. Detailed policy proposals are inherently divisive, they warned. Getting specific would only give the Democrats something to attack. Reagan bristled a bit at that, eager to lay out his plans for the next four years. But in the end he went along with his advisors, who built a campaign around broad, sunny themes. "It's Morning in America." "America Is Back." Reagan didn't love it, but you can't say the strategy didn't work. With an opposition party still fractured from the primary season and a personal-approval rating that approached 70 percent, the truth was that Reagan never really had to break a sweat. Everything was stacked in favor of his reelection, just as everything was stacked *against* the Mondale-Ferraro ticket ... other than an early burst of media coverage celebrating Ferraro's place as the nation's first female major-party vice presidential nominee. Given Reagan's popularity and his achievements over the previous four years, all he really had to do in the 1984 campaign was be Ronald Reagan and answer a few pointed questions about his intentions and his age. And if anyone expected

Mondale to move to the center once the fall campaign began, that prospect was dashed before he ever left San Francisco, when he promised in his acceptance speech to *raise* taxes.

"Whoever is inaugurated in January, the American people will have to pay Mr. Reagan's bills," Mondale asserted from the podium. "The budget will be squeezed. Taxes will go up. And anyone who says they won't is not telling the truth to the American people. . . . Mr. Reagan will raise taxes, and so will I. He won't tell you. I just did."

Political professionals have an expression for a strategy like that one. *Stupid and wrongheaded.* And voters reacted just about how you'd expect them to.

Poorly.

For the Reagan-Bush reelection team, there were a few small bumps along the way, including a tiny dust-up on August 11 when Reagan was testing a microphone before a radio broadcast. "I've signed legislation that will outlaw Russia forever," he deadpanned. "We begin bombing in five minutes."

His off-the-cuff joke went public, and not everyone was amused. The Mondale campaign said it proved that Reagan couldn't be trusted to run U.S. foreign policy in the nuclear age. But that only made the Democrats look like hysterics, and most Americans didn't mind that Reagan also had a lighter side. If the big national shrug was any indication, people even liked it.

The age issue was a little trickier. Reagan was seventy-three during the fall campaign. He'd be seventy-four two weeks after Inauguration Day and not quite seventy-eight at the end of his second term. Those numbers may not sound so ancient here in the

Biden-Trump-Hillary era. Eighty wasn't yet the new seventy. But at that point in history, Reagan could still be declared America's oldest president.

Eager to combat any suggestion that he might be losing it mentally, Reagan's aides prepared him rigorously for the first televised debate, on October 7 at the Kentucky Center for the Arts in Louisville. Prepared him and prepared him and prepared him. For weeks before, they crammed his mind with facts and figures. They had him review policy papers and memorize catchphrases. They put him through six—yes, *six*—full-dress rehearsals. The campaign aides did everything they could think of to get Reagan ready for Mondale, who'd spent twelve years in the Senate and four as vice president and had a Washington insider's knowledge of all the ins and outs of the federal bureaucracy. Then they crammed a few more facts into Reagan's head.

The thoroughly predictable upshot: it was the worst debate Ronald Reagan ever had.

His usual comfort on stage seemed to abandon him. A couple of times his mind went momentarily blank. All those facts and figures overwhelmed him. At one point, he even seemed confused about what city he was in. During a discussion of the defense budget he noted the high cost of the military's "food and wardrobe." They had prepared him into a complete state of exhaustion and confusion.

As *New York Times* TV critic John Corry put it, Reagan was "determined to prove that he knew details, and that statistics held no terror. He seemed, however, to pay a price. The turning point in the debate seemed to come when he was asked a question about taxes … It was not a terribly difficult question. But Mr. Reagan prefaced his answer by turning to Mr. Mondale and saying, 'You know, I wasn't going to say this at all, but I can't help it: There you go again.'"

Huh?

That was the catchphrase Reagan had employed four years earlier in the debate with Jimmy Carter. It had worked brilliantly that time. But now it had nothing to do with the question being asked or with anything that Mondale had said. It was an unmoored Reagan floating in a sea of extraneous detail.

The campaign put out the usual rah-rah statements about how well their guy had done. But by the next morning even Reagan had stopped pretending . . . to himself. "Well," he wrote in his diary, "the debate took place & I have to say I lost. I guess I'd crammed so hard on facts & figures in view of the absolutely dishonest things he's been saying in the campaign I guess I flattened out—anyway I didn't feel good about myself."

For the first time, Mondale saw an opening. "Today, we have a brand-new race," the freshly invigorated Democrat declared. That might have been a dose of wishful thinking, but Mondale wasn't totally wrong. The momentum was suddenly going his way. The *Washington Post*-ABC News poll showed he'd narrowed Reagan's lead from 18 points to 12. Had Reagan left an impression he'd have trouble reversing? Was his lead about to narrow even more? To their credit, Reagan's campaign advisors recognized immediately how poorly they had served their candidate, and they didn't try to make excuses for over-preparing him.

"The man was absolutely smothered," said Paul Laxalt, Reagan's campaign chairman and closest friend in the U.S. Senate.

"He was brutalized by a briefing process that didn't make sense," a relentless prep regime that would have been "unfair for a twenty-one-year-old." And all of it only exacerbated the age issue in the public's mind.

Laxalt promised not to repeat the mistake when Reagan and Mondale met two weeks later in Kansas City for their second debate. "This time," the campaign chairman promised, "we're going to let Ronald Reagan be Ronald Reagan."

And so they did.

Well into the second debate, Henry Trewhitt, the diplomatic correspondent for the *Baltimore Sun*, asked a question that was on everyone's mind. "Mr. President," he said, "I want to raise an issue that I think has been lurking out there for two or three weeks and cast it specifically in national-security terms. You already are the oldest president in history. And some of your staff say you were tired after your most recent encounter with Mr. Mondale. I recall yet that President Kennedy had to go for days on end with very little sleep during the Cuban missile crisis. Is there any doubt in your mind that you would be able to function in such circumstances?"

"Not at all, Mr. Trewhitt," Reagan answered. Then he delivered what became the most famous thirty-two words of the 1984 campaign. Said Reagan: "And I want you to know that also I will not make age an issue of this campaign. I am not going to exploit, for political purposes, my opponent's youth and inexperience."

An immediate outburst of applause and laughter filled the hall. Over Reagan's left shoulder in the live TV shot, the fifty-six-year-old Mondale could be seen laughing at Reagan's perfectly crafted punch line. Did that one pointed quip prove that Reagan had the mental clarity and physical vigor to handle everything that might be thrown at him over the next four years? Of course not. It was one line in one debate. But it gave voters the sense that Reagan was still "with it" enough to outmaneuver an experienced Washington figure like Walter Mondale and that the Republican president hadn't lost his natural charm or his good cheer. Four years after he'd first moved into the White House, he still had the common touch that had helped to deliver him there. And at that moment, Mondale would admit later, he knew for certain that the race was over and that the president's reelection was assured.

As predicted, Reagan's poll numbers got a nice bounce after the second debate, and he coasted to easy victory. On Election Day, he carried forty-nine of the fifty states. Mondale's only wins came in the District of Columbia and his home state of Minnesota, where he squeaked ahead by 3,761 votes.

Reagan's win was even more jaw-dropping than his Carter landslide in 1980. An 18-percent margin of victory. A real blowout. Instead of the 489 electoral votes he'd scored four years earlier, it was 525 this time to Mondale's 13. As Reagan woke up in the White House on the last morning of his first term as president, he had a lot to be proud of. His tax cuts had defeated the Carter-era "stagflation," that nagging combination of high unemployment and high inflation. The latest scorecard said that the U.S. economy had grown by 6.8 percent in 1984—the biggest one-year increase in decades. America's place in the world was also much improved. Reagan's moral clarity, military buildup, and Star Wars missile defense plan had put the Soviets suddenly on the defensive. A new wave of patriotism had swept across America. Reagan was seventy-three years, eleven months, and fourteen days old . . . and definitely ready for more.

The low that day was 7 degrees Fahrenheit. With the windchill factor, it felt like minus 20, the TV weather people said. Washington was so bitterly cold on January 20, 1985, Reagan's outdoor inaugural had to be put on ice. The parade up Pennsylvania Avenue was canceled. So was the open-air inaugural address. "There is no way we should inflict this risk on all the people who would have to be out in the cold for hours," Reagan wrote in his diary that day. To begin his second term, he was sworn in twice: once officially, at the White House in front of a grand total of ninety-six people, and then the following day before about a thousand people in the Capitol Rotunda, where Chief Justice Warren Burger administered the oath of office and Jessye Norman sang "Simple Gifts" from Aaron Copland's *Old American Songs*.

Should those cold winds have been taken as a portent for the challenges of the next four years?

Reagan's inaugural address, the one he'd intended to deliver on the steps outside, isn't remembered for its soaring language or its inspiring themes. He jam-packed the speech with all the specifics that his advisors had kept out of the fall campaign, finally laying out his policy agenda for the next four years.

He would ask Congress to pass a balanced budget amendment, he said. He'd seek to restrain non-defense discretionary spending, even more than he already had. "We must simplify our tax system, make it more fair, and bring the rates down for all who work and earn," he said. He made clear that he was still no fan of welfare. The private economy "and support from family and community" was the best way to "reduce dependency and upgrade the dignity of those who are infirm or disadvantaged," he said, terming his private-sector approach the "new American emancipation."

On the world stage, Reagan vowed to press ahead with his Strategic Defense Initiative, nicknamed the "Star Wars" missile defense shield. He promised to renew his efforts for an arms control agreement with the Soviet Union and seek "the total elimination one day of nuclear weapons from the face of the Earth," what he called "global zero." And he promised democracy-building efforts around the world, putting America firmly on the side of people who "hunger for the right of self-determination, for those inalienable rights that make for human dignity and progress." That last point would soon be known as the Reagan Doctrine. He would put some flesh on those bones two weeks later in his State of the Union address, where he declared: "We must not break faith with those who are risking their lives—on every continent from Afghanistan to Nicaragua—to defy Soviet-supported aggression and secure rights which have been ours from birth."

He didn't say explicitly how far he planned to go with that. But White House aides made clear just how sweeping the president's vision was, explaining that he intended to take a far more assertive posture against communist influence around the world. Terms like *rollback* would replace *containment* and *détente*. And American arms could soon be flowing to the contras fighting the leftist government in Nicaragua, to Jonas Savimbi's UNITA guerrillas in Angola, to the mujahideen in Afghanistan, and to other "freedom fighters" in godforsaken corners of the world.

After his massive reelection victory, Reagan felt like he had a solid mandate from the American people to govern . . . *his way.* This time the voters didn't take their chances on someone who'd never held federal office before, as they had four years earlier. By now they'd seen exactly what a Reagan presidency was like and, in record numbers, seemed to be demanding even more of the same.

CHAPTER 12

EVIL EMPIRE

Despite what he thought *and said* about the Soviet Union, Reagan still wanted to negotiate with America's prime adversary. The future of the planet might hang in the balance, he believed. But who exactly was he supposed to talk to?

LESSON LEARNED: KEEP YOUR FRIENDS CLOSE.
KEEP THE RUSSIANS EVEN CLOSER.

Ronald Reagan earned his place in the annals of anti-communism long before he ever got close to the White House.

He'd been identifying as an anti-Communist since his Hollywood years—in part *because of* his Hollywood years. He'd seen how left-leaning actors and behind-the-scenes movie craftspeople (and, especially, some of their union reps) had gotten far too snuggly with Soviet communism. He had no use for socialism, collectivism, leftism, or any of Marxism's other starry-eyed fellow travelers. And when it came to the Soviet Union, there was never any equivocation on Reagan's part. He'd always given the cold shoulder to America's number one enemy in the Cold War.

Those feelings really jelled for him during his General Electric tours, where he made anti-communism a key part of The Speech. And the message grew only stronger when he got to the governor's office, where he battled radicals at Berkeley, stood up to Black Panthers in Oakland, and tangled with liberal Democrats in the California Legislature. To him, America's New Left was nothing more than a repackaged version of the Old Left . . . just with longer hair and with hard-rock anthems instead of Woodie Guthrie songs. "When a conservative says that totalitarian Communism is an absolute enemy of human freedom," Reagan told the CPAC convention in 1977, "he is not theorizing—he is reporting the ugly reality captured so unforgettably in the writings of Alexsandr Solzhenitsyn," the imprisoned Russian dissident.

Reagan saw Soviet communism as a system of cruelty, inefficiency, and regimentation that was not sustainable except by terrible oppression and exploitation, a system that had caused untold damage to its people and the world—truly a system doomed. When his foreign policy advisor Richard Allen brought up the subject of U.S.-Soviet relations in 1977, Reagan answered without missing a beat: "Here's my strategy on the Cold War. We win, they lose." (Note for today's leaders: China needs a similar message.) And when Reagan addressed the British House of Commons after becoming president, he gleefully taunted America's fiercest rival, hijacking a famous phrase from Leon Trotsky at the start of the Russian Revolution. Only now, Reagan turned that phrase on the

Soviet Union. "The march of freedom and democracy," he warned, "will leave Marxism-Leninism on the ash heap of history."

No pulled punches there!

So, how is it that Ronald Reagan ended up sitting down with Soviet leader Mikhail Gorbachev—not once but four times during his presidency? Given Reagan's anti-communist pedigree and Gorbachev's lifelong dedication to the communist cause, how did these two strong-willed leaders ever lock themselves in a room together and hammer out a historic arms control deal? There's an important lesson in here about engaging productively with our most bitter opponents . . . without ever forgetting it's their permanent destruction we are ultimately hoping for.

This would be different from all the other negotiations that Reagan had ever been a part of. Even in his most furious moments when he tried to strike a deal with a senator, a congressman, or a member of the California Legislature or the Screen Actors Guild, Reagan was trying to reach a conclusion that strengthened the institution. He and Jesse Unruh could disagree ferociously about an issue, but they didn't disagree about the need for the California Assembly. Reagan could fight with Tip O'Neill and they could both leave the room twice as angry as when they walked in, but the Democratic House Speaker never wanted the separation of powers scuttled so he didn't have to deal with Reagan ever again. And Reagan didn't want his supporters to, say, storm the Capitol and try to reverse the results of a lawful election. All those efforts sustained and substantiated the democratic process, even if the participants hated the issue-to-issue results. Nobody wanted

America weaker, and certainly none of them wanted American democracy to disappear.

The Gorbachev relationship would be fundamentally different, even as Reagan found things to like and admire about the reform-minded Soviet leader. For the first time in his life, Reagan would be engaged in a negotiation whose ultimate objective was to destroy—in this case, to induce the death of the Soviet Union. He didn't want to give Gorbachev a way out because a way out meant a continued, if tamed, Soviet Union. In his negotiations in L.A., Sacramento, and Washington, the idea was always to bend. With Gorbachev, Reagan's goal was to break. The challenge now was how best to accomplish that with the least amount of disruption and tragedy—and to take care of one little issue in the meantime.

To make sure the planet wasn't incinerated in a nuclear conflagration.

Literally.

Reagan really laid down a marker for America's fiercest rival when he flew to Orlando, Florida, in March of 1983 to address the National Association of Evangelicals. That was the day he introduced the term *evil empire*. By then, the Soviets were four years into their brutal assault on Afghanistan. Their cold war with the United States had been raging for nearly four decades. In case anyone thought Reagan might not really mean *evil*, he also told the evangelicals that the Kremlin was "the focus of evil in the modern world." By choosing such moralistic language, the American president was firmly rejecting the mushy notion, which had grown in popularity, that Moscow and Washington were somehow equally responsible for the escalating arms race and the long-running superpower standoff.

Reagan didn't buy that for an atomic second. And he wasn't shy about putting the U.S.-Soviet conflict in starkly religious terms. "Yes," he said that day, "let us pray for the salvation of all of those who live in that totalitarian darkness—pray they will discover the joy of knowing God. But until they do, let us be aware that while they preach the supremacy of the State, declare its omnipotence over individual man, and predict its eventual domination of all peoples on the earth, they are the focus of evil in the modern world."

The runaway arms race, he added, was more than "a giant misunderstanding." It simply wasn't true that "both sides are equally at fault." This "struggle between right and wrong and good and evil" was propelled by "the aggressive impulses of an evil empire."

The Evil Empire was evil. How much plainer could he be?

But there was still the question of what, if anything, Reagan could do about it in the short run, even as he committed himself to winning the Cold War and seeing that the Soviet Union was ultimately destroyed. He had no idea how long that might take. The balance between these two heavily armed superpowers hadn't changed much in years. Both sides had massive militaries and more nuclear weapons than they could ever think of using. The MAD doctrine of Mutually Assured Destruction meant that each nation had a devastating arsenal pointed at the other but no rational justification for ever launching it. No *rational* justification. Whoever went first, we'd all be blown to smithereens.

So, what was the point of Reagan's rhetoric in Orlando? Was

the Republican president merely pandering to the political pooh-bahs of the Religious Right, some of whom were still smarting over his nomination of Sandra Day O'Connor to the U.S. Supreme Court? No, actually. He was setting the stage to negotiate with his nation's sworn enemy—not over their ultimate future but to make the world a little safer from nuclear annihilation until their evil empire could be finished off once and for all.

As James Miller, who directed Reagan's Office of Management and Budget, put it years later: "He thought MAD was mad. . . . He wanted to reduce the ability of one country to kill another, dramatically." Reagan knew that muscular rhetoric alone would never accomplish that. Nor would military might—not alone. Nearly half a century had proven that. To make immediate progress in protecting America, Reagan understood, he would need to engage—yes, *engage*—with the leaders of the Soviet Union. They had to sit down and talk.

That was the power of face-to-face, something Reagan had proven himself to be a master at. He'd done it with Tip and Jesse and the lefties in Hollywood and come out on top nearly every time. After all that, how hard could a Communist Party secretary really be? Reagan thought the leader of the Free World should at least be trying.

But who exactly was he supposed to talk to?

Reagan couldn't sit down and strike a deal with "the Kremlin." The Kremlin is a building, albeit a symbolically potent one, a fortified complex at the center of the Russian capital that overlooks Red Square and the Moskva River and serves as the official residence of the Russian president. You can't negotiate with *the Kremlin* any more than you can negotiate with *the White House*. Only people can negotiate. And that, right there, was a challenge for Reagan ever since he took office . . . for one simple reason. The aged Soviet leaders kept dying on him.

In the early months of Reagan's presidency, Leonid Brezhnev had already been the general secretary of the Communist Party and chairman of the Presidium of the Supreme Soviet for more than sixteen years. Brezhnev was seventy-four years old—and not a *young* seventy-four. He was in no mood for tackling the complex issue of arms control or fundamentally rethinking his nation's relationship with the United States. Most days, the aging Soviet leader needed a nap. He certainly wasn't looking to tangle with the notorious anti-Communists who'd moved into the White House. And when Brezhnev died in November 1982, it took a couple of tries before a proper replacement could be found.

The sickly Yuri Andropov, Brezhnev's immediate successor, died of kidney failure after fifteen months in office and didn't do much while he was there. He vowed to fight corruption but didn't fight too much of it. He was mostly overwhelmed by the nation's sinking economy and the rising tensions of the Cold War. Andropov's main achievement, in hindsight, was advancing the rise of a young reformer named Mikhail Gorbachev.

Andropov was followed by Konstantin Chernenko, who barely lasted a year. He was so frail, he had trouble reading the eulogy at his predecessor's funeral. Chernenko swallowed his words, coughed repeatedly, and kept stopping to wipe his lips and forehead. No one could hear what he was saying. He rode a newly installed escalator up to Lenin's mausoleum and shuffled down with a bodyguard on either arm. He was soon confined to Central Clinical Hospital with emphysema, heart disease, and other ailments. (He'd been smoking cigarettes since he was nine.) Now he barely had the strength to sign the documents that were faxed over from the Politburo. Even a trip to the mineral baths at Kislovodsk didn't help. He fell into a coma and died on the evening of March 10, 1985, the third Soviet leader to die in less than three years. When Reagan was awakened with the news, the American president didn't miss a beat: "How am I supposed to get anyplace with the Russians if they keep dying on me?"

Good question, Mr. President.

It wasn't until Mikhail Gorbachev got the top job the day after Chernenko's death that the Soviet Union had a younger, more vibrant leader who would stick around long enough to engage in a genuine bilateral dialogue—and Reagan would finally get a legitimate dance partner on the world stage. Gorbachev had just turned fifty-four.

By the standards of the hidebound Soviet Politburo, he was known as relatively open-minded. That might not be saying much, but it sure beat the recent alternatives. His CIA file said he'd raised early doubts in the Central Committee about the Soviet invasion of Afghanistan. After Brezhnev's death, he had advocated for some liberal reforms, which went exactly nowhere under Andropov and Chernenko. Gorbachev was also a whole generation younger than the fossils he had just replaced. And he got promising reviews from Reagan's friend Margaret Thatcher. The conservative British prime minister had invited Gorbachev to London just before he took on the general secretary's role. At the end of the visit, Thatcher said: "I like Mr. Gorbachev. We can do business together."

Reagan was eager to take that theory for a test drive.

It had been more than six years since the last superpower summit, when Jimmy Carter met with Brezhnev in Vienna and nothing much was achieved. A lot had happened since then. The détente of the 1970s had long since evaporated. The SALT II arms control treaty had collapsed. The Soviet Union invaded Afghanistan, which provoked the 1980 Olympic boycott. Crises had worsened in Nicaragua, Iran, and the Horn of Africa. In the absence of face-to-face interaction at the highest levels of the two governments, the usual Cold War tensions had gotten noticeably worse. But at least now there was someone to talk to.

Admittedly, there was good reason for skepticism about how far this might go. The Soviets had, of course, heard all of Reagan's trash talk about them. Branding someone else's country an "evil empire" isn't usually the best foot to get off on in a challenging negotiation. The term doesn't exactly convey *Let's see if you and I can work something out together.* But Gorbachev didn't seem at all put off by Reagan's bluntness, even if he vehemently disagreed with its conclusion. And Reagan was hopeful that, once the two men got down to business, they might actually find some areas of agreement.

Both sides had plenty to gain, even beyond a desire to avoid blowing up the planet (though that *was* a good reason) and even as they both wished for each other's ultimate destruction. Russia was going broke paying its arms race bills. All those T-14 Armata tanks and Sukhoi Su-57 fighter jets weren't putting borscht and

beef Stroganoff on dinner tables across the Soviet republics . . . or
buying anyone a special-occasion bottle of Belenkaya vodka. The
people needed food, shelter, technology, and all the other things
that made life worth living in a cold, dark, sprawling, late-term
statist empire. As long as the Soviet government was locked in an
endless quest for military superiority against the wealthier United
States, Gorbachev knew that his people would continue to suffer,
denied too many of the comforts and luxuries that the citizens of
other nations were able to enjoy. Gorbachev wasn't about to shrink
his troop strength, any more than Reagan was going to shrink his.
But what about all those nuclear weapons? Wasn't there room for
trimming there?

The two leaders met for the first time in Geneva, Switzerland, on
November 19 and 20, 1985, eight months after Gorbachev assumed
office. What an improbable pair they made! The capitalist and the
communist. The American and the Russian. The friend of freedom
everywhere and the leader of the nation that held an iron grip on a
wide swath of Eastern Europe, not to mention its own oppressed
people and assorted other client states around the world. Still, Reagan thought it was important to establish a personal connection
right away before getting down to the nitty-gritty of throw weights
and warhead counts.

"The United States and the Soviet Union are the two greatest
countries on Earth, the superpowers," Reagan said as soon as the
two men shook hands. "We are the only two countries who can start
World War III but also the only two countries that can bring peace

to the world." Then he marveled at how much he and Gorbachev had in common, both coming from "rural hamlets in the middle of our respective countries" and what a profound responsibility now rested on their shoulders.

Classic Reagan. He was able to pound Gorbachev from a distance with "evil empire" rhetoric while at the same time charming him up close with his warmth and storytelling style. It had served him in Hollywood, Sacramento, and the halls of Congress. Now he was giving it a try at the Geneva summit. And having set the stage with that rhetorical punch in the face, Reagan now had wider leeway in negotiating with the Soviets—much more than Walter Mondale or some other temperate Democrat would have had—with the political capital to explore a meaningful, bilateral deal. And he seized on it.

During one of the early breaks, the two leaders took a walk with just their translators so they could speak more candidly about the issues facing their countries. Gorbachev later revealed the question that Reagan asked him on that walk: "What would you do if the United States were suddenly attacked by aliens from outer space? Would you help us?"

"No doubt about it," the Soviet leader said.

"Us too," Reagan assured him.

"So that's interesting . . . ," Gorbachev mused aloud, as he tried to get his head around the meaning of that unexpected exchange. Then both men burst out laughing.

If some incalculable outside force should threaten either nation, the other *would* be inclined to step up if that's what it took to protect the world. Was it too much to hope that these two sworn enemies really might come together as allies as they had against the Nazis in World War II? No matter how far-fetched Reagan's hypothetical, he was laying a foundational concept. It was just a short leap from there to the real threat that somehow needed to be managed: the threat of nuclear annihilation.

It certainly took the conversation out of the usual foreign policy box. And it must have worked to some extent: their first meeting went an hour and a half longer than it was scheduled to.

That day and the next, the two leaders nibbled around the edges of a wide variety of issues, phony and real: short- and medium-range nuclear weapons ... the Strategic Defense Initiative missile shield Reagan wanted to build over parts of the United States ... the Soviets' oppression of their own people ... sexism in America. (That's right, Gorbachev gave a passionate shout-out to American feminists, women he said he'd always admired.) Some of this was dead serious, and some of it was just for show back home. Like a couple of prizefighters in the early rounds of a bout, the two rivals seemed to be testing each other's limits and gauging what reactions to expect. But as the two-day summit came to a close, there wasn't anything much to announce except that they would keep talking, which after six years of silence was an achievement in itself, assuming the fifty-four-year-old Russian leader's health held out long enough to proceed.

Worrisome data point number 1: Average life expectancy for an adult Russian male in the mid-1980s: 58 years. Worrisome data point number 2: Average vodka consumption for an adult Russian male in the mid-1980s: 180 bottles a year, a half bottle every single day.

Well, at least Reagan and Gorbachev knew each other now.

• • •

The dealmaking heated up in Iceland. Or did it? It was hard to say.

When Reagan and Gorbachev arrived in Reykjavík on October 11, 1986, for their second superpower summit, they were clearly buoyed by the friendly familiarity of their nice-to-meet-you sit-down in Switzerland. But good feelings alone would not produce a nuclear agreement between these two sworn enemies. That would take hard negotiation, a little flexibility, a lot of creativity, and maybe even some humility across the international divide.

Good luck with that.

The whole world was waiting to see if these two strong-willed individuals, so different from each other in so many ways, could actually find some middle ground. Would Reagan's charm and clarity move the stubborn Gorbachev? Would Gorbachev's assurances of next-generation openness move the skeptical Reagan? If so, could this unlikely pair actually leave Iceland with a deal?

Well, they tried.

Gorbachev proposed banning various classes of nuclear weapons. Reagan wanted to continue research on his high-tech missile shield, which Gorbachev derided as the Star Wars militarization of outer space. (Back to those aliens again?) Reagan wanted to discuss human rights, the emigration of Soviet Jews and dissidents, and the Soviet invasion of Afghanistan. Gorbachev didn't want to talk about any of that. He wanted the discussion focused on arms control. They poked. They prodded. They traded little insults. Reagan proposed eliminating intermediate-range missiles in Europe. Gorbachev suggested cutting 50 percent of the longer-range ICBMs.

But all that was contingent on the Americans postponing Star Wars for at least ten years, and Reagan wouldn't agree to that. In the end, the two leaders mostly talked past each other. Reagan trotted out fresh loads of his legendary charm—and some old-fashioned American nudging—in hopes of pushing a deal across the finish line. Did Gorbachev really want to "turn down this historic opportunity?" But Gorbachev hung tough. This time the charm offensive fell short. And after ten hours of intense pushing and pulling, the negotiations ended right there. The best the two sides could manage on their way out the door was the same thing they had achieved the last time: an agreement to meet again in both of their capitals, Washington first and then Moscow.

Yes, all this talking was nice. But no one could answer the much larger question: Could these two ever make a deal?

CHAPTER 13

CHALLENGED

When the space shuttle *Challenger* exploded off the coast of Florida, killing everyone aboard, Reagan knew he'd soon be speaking to the people of America. What he quickly came to realize was that he'd also be speaking *for* them.

LESSON LEARNED:
LEADERS START WHERE THE PEOPLE ARE.

Winter hit the east coast of Florida like a cold slap in the face.

The overnight low was a frigid 18.6 degrees Fahrenheit, light-years from the fifties and low sixties that January typically brings. The temperature at launch time was a brisk 26. The sky above Cape Canaveral was a steely, hopeful blue. There'd been some concern about ice formation, but the NASA flight engineers—and there are no better engineers *anywhere*—said not to worry. They'd taken steps to minimize the crystal buildup, and in any event it wasn't a threat to the safety of the mission or the crew.

Five men and two women were going up on the space shuttle

Challenger. But Christa McAuliffe was the one who had generated by far the most excitement. A thirty-seven-year-old high school social studies teacher from Concord, New Hampshire, and the mother of two young children, Christa was selected from applicants for NASA's Teacher in Space Project. She'd undergone months of training. She'd be conducting experiments and teaching two lessons in space, part of the mission's larger purpose, which included deploying a communications satellite and studying Halley's Comet.

For the past six days, she and her fellow crew members had waited anxiously at the Kennedy Space Center while the launch was delayed and delayed and delayed because of high winds, a frozen hatch handle, and other weather and technical difficulties. That's space travel. You go when you can go. But at last the moment was here. The seven astronauts were all strapped in, moving through their preflight protocols, finally ready for liftoff. Mission STS-51-L would be the tenth trip for the partly reusable *Challenger* and the twenty-fifth flight of the space shuttle fleet. Now this high school teacher and mom of two was about to become the first civilian ever to travel into space. The date was Tuesday, January 28, 1986. Launch time was 11:38 a.m.

Hugh Harris, the veteran voice of launch control, began the familiar countdown in his usual, methodical way.

"T-minus ten, nine, eight . . ."

At Concord High in New Hampshire, where 26 degrees is nothing, Mrs. McAuliffe had been talking about her upcoming adventure since everyone returned from summer vacation. TVs were on in many of the classrooms. The students could hardly wait for their teacher to blast into space. She'd promised to tell them everything just as soon as she got back home.

"Seven, six . . . we have main engine start."

Christa's husband, Steven, and their son and daughter, nine-year-old Scott and six-year-old Caroline, had come to Florida to witness the liftoff firsthand. Bundled against the cold Florida morning, Christa's parents, Ed and Grace Corrigan, were also there. So was her sister, Lisa. They were in an open-air grandstand four miles from the launchpad, set aside for relatives and guests of the crew members. Eighteen students from Concord High had also made the trip. They, too, watched with pride and nervous excitement as the countdown continued, relieved that the moment had finally arrived.

"Four, three, two, one . . . and liftoff. Liftoff of the twenty-fifth space shuttle mission, and it has cleared the tower."

And up *Challenger* went, hurled into the sky on the ferocious thrust of its three Phase I engines, trailed by a giant plume of flame and smoke from the aft end of the orbiter, soon to be joined by the earsplitting staccato of the twin solid rocket boosters as they kicked in.

Hugh Harris passed off to Space Center Houston. The mission's flight-monitoring team picked up the play-by-play from there. "*Challenger* now heading down range. . . . Engines beginning throttling down now. . . . At ninety-four percent. Normal throttle for most of the flight, one hundred and four percent. We'll throttle down to sixty-five percent shortly."

The team in Houston ticked calmly through the post-launch checklist.

"Three engines running normally.... Three good fuel cells....
Three good A.U.P.... Velocity 2,257 feet per second.... Altitude,
four-point-three nautical miles.... Downrange distance three nautical miles.... Engines throttling up.... Three engines now at one-
oh-four percent."

Sitting at the ground team's capcom console, Dick Covey
relayed a routine directive to flight commander Dick Scobee:
"*Challenger*, go at throttle up."

"Roger," Scobee radioed back. "Go at throttle up."

Not a hint of danger in any of this as 51-L achieved an altitude
of nine miles over the Atlantic Ocean, traveling at almost twice the
speed of sound.

Not for the first seventy-three seconds, there wasn't, not that
anyone on the ground or in the air could detect.

Then *this*:

A giant burst of white smoke suddenly appeared where the
accelerating spacecraft had been. A muffled clap could be heard
from the viewing grandstand where the relatives stood. There was
no craft hurling through the sky anymore, just some large, silent
corkscrews of bright white smoke against the flat blue sky and then
a massive hailstorm of debris falling into the ocean below.

Some of this was hard to see from the ground. Peering into the
morning sky, the spectators needed time to grasp the full extent of
the catastrophe unfolding above them. It would take another few
seconds before they began to absorb the true horror of it all. But
that dreadful realization spread across the crowd in little bursts.

Some people were still cheering. Others held their fists in the
air, flashing thumbs-up victory signs. But the exuberant looks on

people's faces were melting now. Jaws dropping. Heads shaking. Stunned silence. Grimaces where smiles had been.

What the—? A lot of people still appeared genuinely confused.

There was still no alarm in the voices from Houston as the monitoring team continued the play-by-play. But their message had turned dire.

"Flight controller here, looking very carefully at the situation.... Obviously a major malfunction.... We have a report from the flight dynamics officer that the vehicle has exploded. Flight director confirms that. We are looking at, uh, checking with the recovery forces to see what can be done at this point.... Contingency procedures are in effect. We will report more as we have information available.... Again, to repeat, we have a report replayed through the flight dynamics officer that the vehicle has exploded. We are now looking at all the contingency operations, awaiting word from any recovery operations in the downrange field."

On the ground in Florida, Christa's sister, Lisa, grabbed her father's hand, while Christa's mother laid her head on her husband's shoulder. On his sweater was a large button with Christa's smiling face. That's when someone from NASA came over and put into words what the family members were only then starting to process.

"The craft has exploded," he said.

Christa's mom repeated the words to her husband as screams and loud cries broke out around them. It was a reaction already being echoed across the country as word of the *Challenger* disaster quickly spread everywhere and the shock gave way to horror and the rattled people of a shaken nation tried to figure out how to grieve.

. . . .

Ronald Reagan wasn't watching television when the *Challenger* blew up. His schedule was too packed that day.

He started with an early-morning staff meeting, then joined a session with congressional leaders. "Had a go around with Tip—think I came out pretty good," he noted later. Then it was a quick grip-and-grin with Alaska senator Frank Murkowski and a very nice family who'd recently been reunited in the United States: an American husband, Vietnamese wife, and their two young children. After that, the president began a briefing before a long-planned luncheon with Tom Brokaw, Dan Rather, Peter Jennings, and other network-TV anchors to preview the State of the Union address, which was scheduled for 9:00 that night.

Reagan and his aides were trading ideas—no anchors yet—when Vice President Bush rushed in with National Security Advisor John Poindexter. The space shuttle *Challenger* had exploded in Florida shortly after takeoff. All seven crew members were killed. The pre-lunch briefing ended immediately. Reagan, Bush, and Poindexter moved into the small dining room off the Oval Office, where the TV was already on. Soon the group also included chief of staff Donald Regan, communications director Patrick Buchanan, cabinet secretary Alfred Kingon, and deputy press secretary Edward Djerejian—all of them in dark suits and ties, staring glumly at the wall-to-wall coverage that had just taken over the news.

Even Reagan was momentarily at a loss for words. "There is no way to describe our shock & horror," he wrote in his diary that day. "We cancelled—I should say postponed the St. of the Union address till next week. Cong. closed down for the day."

For Reagan, space was a lifelong dream. Like many children of the prairie, he'd looked up at bright, starry nights and wondered what—or who—might be up there. As air travel grew more routine, there was always the question of what was even higher than where the planes went. Ever since he got to the White House, Reagan had been trying to bring new energy to the space program, which had lost some of its focus and its sizzle, not to mention some of its congressional funding, since the heady, walk-on-the-moon days of the Apollo missions.

Reagan considered outer space a place of opportunity for America and humanity's final frontier. Having spent all those years in California and having starred in half a dozen Westerns—*Law and Order, The Last Outpost, Cowboy from Brooklyn, Cattle Queen of Montana, Tennessee's Partner, Santa Fe Trail*—he had an innate understanding of the potent mythology of the American frontier. To his way of thinking, space was the next frontier that needed exploring. Like the wagon trains of old had once pressed west, wasn't it America's manifest destiny to now sink roots Up There? His optimism and belief in American exceptionalism guided him the rest of the way. Even as a fiscal conservative hesitant to increase the NASA budget, Reagan's enthusiasm for the topic had commentators calling him America's most pro-space president yet. For a man with a legendary dislike for flying, it was an even larger leap. Space was something he was willing to spend on.

In his 1984 State of the Union, he called for a permanently

crewed international space station, welcoming not just America's allies but the Soviet Union as well, "so we can strengthen peace, build prosperity, and expand freedom for all who share our goals." In June of 1985, Reagan hosted ten finalists from NASA's Teacher in Space Project at the White House. The ten included Christa McAuliffe.

NASA officials believed that having a teacher aboard a future trip—a regular American schoolteacher—might deliver just the burst of attention the space program needed to get people excited again. In a way, that teacher would be a stand-in for all Americans, demonstrating the space shuttle's capabilities and convincing lawmakers to loosen the purse strings a bit.

Reagan praised the teachers for their enthusiasm and asked about their high-flying dreams. He wished them luck on any future voyages and shared what turned out to be an eerily prescient quip. "Whichever of you is chosen," he said, "might also want to take under consideration the opinion of another expert: The acceleration which must result from the use of rockets would damage the brain. So consider yourselves forewarned!"

Classic Reagan humor, not trying to be hilarious, just tossing off a jocular riposte. The teachers took it good-naturedly. He couldn't possibly have known what the future held for one of them. It was later that month that Vice President Bush announced that Christa McAuliffe had been chosen as the prime candidate to be the first civilian in space. A runner-up, Barbara Morgan, was also named in case she was needed. Both of them began training with Commander Dick Scobee and the professional astronauts who filled out his crew: pilot Mike Smith; mission specialists Ellison Onizuka, Judy Resnik, and Ron McNair; and payload specialist

Greg Jarvis. But Christa wasn't going to miss this opportunity, and she didn't.

As the *Challenger* tragedy sunk in for Reagan and he watched the video replay over and over again, he understood how important it was that he address the American people. He'd already been planning to give a speech that night, but this one was even more important. Instead of a laundry list of the nation's goals and accomplishments, he'd be trying to capture something that was in the American people's hearts.

Not simply address a time of pain and upset, but to give meaning to what had happened that day. Give words to what they were feeling. Maybe even offer an early road map out of the grief. It wasn't the number who died in the *Challenger* explosion. We'd lost bigger numbers in wars and natural disasters. It wasn't just the pain their loved ones felt. Loved ones always feel pain. It was all that and more. It was the sudden, unexpected deaths, on national television, of seven brave Americans who'd been carrying the hopes and achievements of a grateful nation into the highest heights of space.

There was no turning away, for America or for Reagan.

When he addressed the American people later that afternoon, Reagan knew, he wouldn't be speaking only as a politician or a president or even the commander in chief. He'd be speaking as a pained fellow American with the awesome responsibility of explaining the unexplainable. And he also had to speak to the children, many of whom just hours earlier had been in classrooms and school auditoriums, witnessing the devastating disaster in real time. He had to, in his words, "make it plain to them that life does go on and you don't back up and quit some worthwhile endeavor because of tragedy."

Chief of Staff Donald Regan asked Peggy Noonan to help. A junior speechwriter with a tiny desk in the Old Executive Office Building, she had a brilliant touch and she totally "got" Reagan's simple, human storytelling style. And time was so short, none of Reagan's senior, less articulate staffers had time to suck the life out of her prose.

The *Challenger* speech was less than five minutes long, so it's easy to quote from end to end. That also saves me from the difficult duty of cutting this perfect line or that one. I don't even mind repeating a couple of lines I quoted before. That's how potent they are. He spoke from the Oval Office at 5:00 p.m.

"Ladies and gentlemen," he said,

I'd planned to speak to you tonight to report on the state of the Union, but the events of earlier today have led me to change those plans. Today is a day for mourning and remembering. Nancy and I are pained to the core by the tragedy of the shuttle *Challenger*. We know we share this pain with all of the people of our country. This is truly a national loss.

Nineteen years ago, almost to the day, we lost three astronauts in a terrible accident on the ground. But we've never lost an astronaut in flight. We've never had a tragedy like this. And perhaps we've forgotten the courage it took for the crew of the shuttle. But they, the *Challenger* Seven, were aware of the dangers, overcame them, and did their jobs brilliantly. We mourn seven heroes: Michael Smith, Dick Scobee, Judith Resnik, Ronald McNair, Ellison Onizuka, Gregory Jarvis, and Christa McAuliffe. We mourn their loss as a nation together.

To the families of the seven, we cannot bear, as you do, the full impact of this tragedy. But we feel the loss, and we're thinking about you so very much. Your loved ones were daring and brave, and they had that special grace, that special spirit that says, "Give me a challenge, and I'll meet it with joy." They had a hunger to explore the universe and discover its truths. They wished to serve, and they did. They served all of us.

We've grown used to wonders in this century. It's hard to dazzle us. But for twenty-five years the United States space program has been doing just that. We've grown used to the idea of space, and perhaps we forget that we've only just begun. We're still pioneers. They, the members of the *Challenger* crew, were pioneers.

And I want to say something to the schoolchildren of America who were watching the live coverage of the shuttle's takeoff. I know it is hard to understand, but sometimes painful things like this happen. It's all part of the process of exploration and discovery. It's all part of taking a chance and expanding man's horizons. The future doesn't belong to the fainthearted. It belongs to the brave. The *Challenger* crew was pulling us into the future, and we'll continue to follow.

I've always had great faith in and respect for our space

program, and what happened today does nothing to diminish it. We don't hide our space program. We don't keep secrets and cover things up. We do it all up front and in public. That's the way freedom is, and we wouldn't change it for a minute.

We'll continue our quest in space. There will be more shuttle flights and more shuttle crews and, yes, more volunteers, more civilians, more teachers in space. Nothing ends here. Our hopes and our journeys continue.

I want to add that I wish I could talk to every man and woman who works for NASA or who worked on this mission and tell them: "Your dedication and professionalism have moved and impressed us for decades. And we know of your anguish. We share it."

There's a coincidence today. On this day 390 years ago, the great explorer Sir Francis Drake died aboard ship off the coast of Panama. In his lifetime, the great frontiers were the oceans, and an historian later said, "He lived by the sea, died on it, and was buried in it." Well, today we can say of the *Challenger* crew: Their dedication was, like Drake's, complete.

The crew of the space shuttle honored us by the manner in which they lived their lives. We will never forget them, nor the last time we saw them, this morning, as they prepared for their journey and waved goodbye and "slipped the surly bonds of earth" to "touch the face of God."

Thank you.

•   •   •

So, what made that speech so moving and so effective? Here's the surprising part. Reagan wasn't happy with it at all.

Recalled speechwriter Noonan: "Reagan left the Oval Office after the speech feeling it had not succeeded. In the words of Abraham Lincoln, he felt it 'hadn't scoured.' Lincoln said a good speech *scours*. It breaks up the earth. Reagan did not feel that the speech had met the moment."

Feeding off her boss's disappointment, Noonan was disappointed too.

Then the reviews started coming in. The calls from regular Americans, including children. They loved it. The messages from people on Capitol Hill. So did they. The media, across the political spectrum, couldn't stop praising the eloquence of Reagan's words, many of the commentators flipping Reagan's self-assessment on its head. The speech "met the moment," they all agreed.

And soon enough, Reagan liked it too.

"By the next morning," Noonan said, "he saw it in a different light. He said, 'There was a heckuva lot of response.' And then he said: 'And Frank Sinatra called me, and I gotta tell you, Frank Sinatra didn't call after every speech!'"

So, what made it work? What did all those people love that Reagan came to love too? Reading that speech now, it's easy to see. He started where the American people were—and took it from there. Grief was the beginning, not the end.

He remembered the dead who were now being celebrated, saying their names out loud. Those weren't just astronauts who died in that terrible explosion. They were individual people too. In the tragedy of these deaths, Reagan found a higher calling for all of us.

After embracing the sadness that everyone was feeling, he broadened to the larger call these American heroes were answering that day. To learn. To explore. To risk. To soar. To go as far and as high as their brains and their bravery would take them. To accept all the challenge of *Challenger* and press nobly on.

Reagan spoke directly to the children, as he knew he had to, and delivered a special message to them. "The future doesn't belong to the fainthearted," as he put it. "It belongs to the brave."

For all ages, he found something greater in the tragedy: even in sadness, the continuing need to soar.

The investigation of the *Challenger* explosion would begin immediately and continue for years. NASA needed to understand exactly what happened. Otherwise, it or something like it could easily happen again. The investigators focused on O-rings and ruptured seals and the frigid temperatures as a contributing factor. Changes were made to equipment, to testing, to training, and to mission profile. But one thing didn't change: NASA's—and America's—quest to conquer space. All these years later, hardly anyone can remember the technical issues anymore. But who can forget a president's moving words?

"We know we share this pain with all of the people of our country. This is truly a national loss. . . . We'll continue our quest in space. There will be more shuttle flights and more shuttle crews and, yes, more volunteers, more civilians, more teachers in space. Nothing ends here. Our hopes and our journeys continue."

And they did.

CHAPTER 14

NEW AMERICANS

Everyone agreed the U.S. immigration system was a mess. Everyone agreed something had to be done. But it was Reagan who put his own law-and-order credentials on the line to act. That wasn't politics. In his mind, it was the right thing to do.

LESSON LEARNED: SOMETIMES, SURPRISE EVERYONE.

He said ... *what?*

All these years later, Ronald Reagan's words can still surprise people. What he said about immigration has been surprising some of his biggest fans for nearly forty years.

"I believe in the idea of amnesty for those who have put down roots and who have lived here, even though sometime back they may have entered illegally."

That quote is from Reagan's final debate with Walter Mondale, two weeks before winning reelection in that forty-nine-state blowout. Asked about U.S. immigration policy, he expressed strong empathy for America's newcomers, no matter how they got here.

And he didn't shy away from using a certain A-word that, in more recent times, would become so toxic in American politics.

Amnesty.

Reagan was for it, he made clear that night in Kansas City . . . as long as certain conditions were met.

Paying a fine and back taxes.

Staying out of trouble.

Learning basic English.

At which point these undocumented immigrants would be fully legalized.

Wait! Wasn't Reagan supposed to be a law-and-order conservative? What's all this amnesty talk?

What made him steaming mad, he told debate questioner Georgie Anne Geyer and the evening's 67 million viewers, were private companies or anyone else trying to take advantage of these vulnerable immigrants. "Employers down through the years have encouraged the illegal entry into this country because they then hire these individuals and hire them at starvation wages and with none of the benefits that we think are normal and natural for workers in our country," Reagan said. "The individuals can't complain because of their illegal status."

That had to stop, he said.

None of this meant that Reagan was for wide-open borders or for ignoring the nation's immigration laws. "It is true our borders are out of control," he said during the debate with Mondale. "It is also true that this has been a situation on our borders back through a number of administrations. . . . I'm going to do everything I can, and all of us in the administration are, to join in again when Congress is back at it to get an immigration bill that will give us, once again, control of our borders." But border security was only part of the equation, he argued. A comprehensive immigration policy also had to include sanctions against sleazy employers, economic aid for Latin America, and a path to legalization for the bulk of those already here.

"No administration that I know has established the relationship that we have with our Latin friends," he said. "But as long as they have an economy that leaves so many people in dire poverty and unemployment, they are going to seek that employment across our borders."

And now he was more than ready to do something about it.

One of the things that makes Reagan still so interesting is that his views and passions were more than a collection of predictable talking points. He thought for himself. He learned from his life experiences. On a multifaceted issue like immigration, he was willing to respond in deeply nuanced ways. And with his own supporters, his bedrock conservatism gave him the leeway to do that.

To admire and learn from Reagan doesn't require agreeing with every single view he held. Issues shift. Times change. And let's be honest, life would be pretty boring if we were all required to sing from the same hymnal. Reagan was the single most towering figure in modern-day conservatism. Not the faux conservatism practiced today by phony poseurs like Donald Trump. The real deal. Both

Reagan and Trump started as Democrats, true. But the Democratic Party shifted left and moved from Reagan. Trump faked a move to the right for reasons of political opportunism. Very different.

Many people, including many Reagan supporters, assume he must have been staunchly opposed to illegal immigration—and in many ways he was. But he was also brimming with personal compassion and informed by the lessons of his own life. He was no open-borders liberal. But he was also no pretend-to-build-a-wall fake conservative. On immigration, he was something we don't have much of anymore: a political leader who saw right and wrong on *both* sides. How Reagan got there is a fascinating story and a never-ending subject of debate.

There is no doubting Reagan's law-and-order credentials. He earned that credibility across the decades. But in his view, immigration was more than an enforcement issue. It was also a social issue, an economic issue, and a fairness issue that went right to the history and the soul of our country. Growing up in small-town Illinois and working as a young man in neighboring Iowa, he'd seen hardworking immigrant families struggling to make their way in America. He'd witnessed something similar when he got to California, where recent immigrants—not all of them legal—toiled on farms, in factories, in restaurants, on construction sites, even in his own movie and television industries. In 1979, just as he was planning to run for president again, Reagan had a private meeting with President José López Portillo of Mexico. On the issue of immigration, the future president was already thinking broad thoughts. Right before the meeting, Reagan wrote in his diary that he hoped to discuss how the United States and Mexico could make the border "something other than the location for a fence." In June of 1981, five months into Reagan's first term, López Portillo came to lunch at the White House. This time he didn't come alone. Sitting with the two presidents was Fernando Valenzuela, a twenty-year-old Mexican-born pitcher in his first full season with the Los Angeles Dodgers, who was just then skyrocketing from obscurity to baseball stardom. Valenzuela's pitching was almost otherworldly. Lifelong fans like Reagan had never seen anything like it. The chubby rookie with a shaggy bush of dark hair won his first eight starts that season, five of them shutouts, and would become the only major leaguer ever to receive the Cy Young and Rookie of the Year Awards in the same season.

Valenzuela didn't speak much English. But through a translator he told Reagan that he came from a tiny town called Etchohuaquila in the Mexican state of Sonora and that he was very excited to see all the famous monuments in Washington. When the conversation turned to immigration, the talented young player said he'd been permitted to work legally in the United States, though many of his friends and relatives back home hadn't been so lucky and they struggled greatly. "My dream was to play baseball in the major leagues," he said. "And now here I am, between two presidents in the White House." Reagan seemed genuinely moved, and so were others who were there that day. After lunch, Vice President George Bush, Secretary of State Alexander Haig, and Defense Secretary Caspar Weinberger all waited patiently while the young pitcher autographed a baseball for each of them.

So many years later, it's impossible to say exactly what impact that lunch might have had on Reagan's long-term thinking about immigration. But afterward he asked his political advisors about reforming U.S. immigration law. His pollsters warned him that most Americans did not support amnesty for people in the country illegally, adding that many of those immigrants would probably vote for Democrats if they ever got the chance. But Reagan kept bringing up the issue, and when his aides speculated about why, they often used the same phrase.

"The Fernando factor."

On a deeper, human level, Reagan seemed to understand why poor people would do almost anything to improve their lives and that of their struggling families.

Reagan was never for open borders. He didn't like seeing people breaking the nation's immigration laws. He knew that created security risks, allowed more undocumented workers to be mistreated, and was unfair to those around the world who were waiting their turn in line. But growing up how he did and living the life he had lived, he focused as much on the people as on the law. And that set him apart from many politicians, on the left and the right, then and now, who have grown so wedded to their own partisan outlooks on the issue of immigration that they can almost never find their way onto middle ground.

So they abhor any compromise and achieve absolutely nothing at all.

Washington's big immigration story of the mid-1980s was a bipartisan proposal called the Simpson-Mazzoli bill, which was slowly twisting and turning its way through Congress. Co-sponsored by Republican senator Alan Simpson of Wyoming and Democratic congressman Romano Mazzoli of Kentucky, the idea was to accomplish several major goals at once: tighten security at the southern border, punish employers who hired undocumented workers, increase aid to Latin America, and also legalize most of the immigrants who had arrived illegally prior to 1982. If passed, Simpson-Mazzoli would be the most sweeping overhaul of U.S. immigration policy since 1952 and 1965. But first the Republican Senate and Democratic House had to agree on the language and details, and that was a maddening process. The bill was introduced, withdrawn, and introduced again. Various drafts were written. Amendments were hung from the bill like Christmas tree ornaments. Almost everyone didn't like something. The two sponsors chaired important immigration subcommittees. So if anyone could, they were in the best possible position to get something done, especially since the president was on their side. But the legislative process was even more bruising than usual, as civil rights activists, business organizations, agricultural interests, Hispanic groups, and, it seemed, just about every lobbyist on K Street all weighed in, trying to yank the bill in one direction or another. Some thought it was too weak. Some thought it was too strong. Some hated the whole idea of "comprehensive." But with the president's firm support, the reform bill finally got across the congressional finish line 63 to 24 in the Republican-controlled Senate, 238 to 173 in the Democratic-controlled House.

"These kinds of bills are really hard to pass," said Charles

Kamasaki, a senior cabinet advisor at the Hispanic civil rights group UnidosUS who wrote a book on the battle titled *Immigration Reform: The Corpse That Will Not Die*. "Before they pass, they almost invariably die. You have to be in a constant search for where you can get the votes. And that inevitably involves tradeoffs and compromises that aren't necessarily fully satisfactory to either side."

"It took a popular president like Reagan to make it happen," agreed Muzaffar Chishti, a senior fellow at the Migration Policy Institute, who lobbied heavily on the bill. Reagan, he marveled, "not only could tell his own party what to do, but he could also tell a significant number of Democrats what to do."

It might have pained them to say it, but even pro-immigration liberals like Kamasaki and Chishti had to give Reagan their grudging respect.

No one seemed happier with the bill's passage than the president who'd pushed so hard for it. Though he took some grief from fellow conservatives, he believed he'd finally achieved what past presidents hadn't been able to: a broad-based deal that could answer several problems at once and would begin a whole new chapter in U.S. immigration policy. Two days after his landslide reelection, a buoyed Reagan called everyone into the Roosevelt Room at the White House and signed what was now officially known as the Immigration Reform and Control Act of 1986.

"Future generations of Americans will be thankful for our efforts to humanely regain control of our borders and thereby preserve the value of one of the most sacred possessions of our people, American citizenship," Reagan said that day.

He made clear he didn't love everything about the bill he had just signed. His staff put out a four-page statement detailing his reservations about certain provisions, including one authored by liberal Democratic congressman Barney Frank of Massachusetts. It outlawed job discrimination against *legal* aliens. Reagan made clear he wouldn't be going overboard enforcing that. He said he would first require solid proof that an employer had shown "discriminatory intent." Yes, he was still Ronald Reagan, suspicious as always about fresh regulations on business. And he wasn't the only one with lingering doubts.

"The bill is a gamble, a riverboat gamble," said future Senate majority leader Chuck Schumer, then a congressman from Brooklyn. "There is no guarantee that employer sanctions will work or that amnesty will work. We are headed into uncharted waters."

Even co-sponsor Alan Simpson agreed nothing was guaranteed. "I don't know what the impact will be," the Republican senator from Wyoming said at the signing ceremony. "But this is the humane approach to immigration reform." To that end, all of them, like Reagan, agreed that the time had finally come for major immigration reform. And the president wasn't backing down an inch from his support for large-scale amnesty.

"The legalization provisions in this act will go far to improve the lives of a class of individuals who now must hide in the shadows, without access to many of the benefits of a free and open society," he said. "Very soon many of these men and women will be able to step into the sunlight and, ultimately, if they choose, they may become Americans."

Three million immigrants applied for amnesty under the new law. Two-point-seven million were accepted into the program. That was well over half of the estimated undocumented population at the time.

They registered, paid their fines and back taxes, and met the other requirements. They showed they could speak English, were of "good moral character," and hadn't been in serious criminal trouble since arriving in the United States. They didn't get instant citizenship, but they got green cards, giving them the legal right to work and putting them on a path that one day might lead—*might* lead— to becoming naturalized citizens. They came out of the shadows, just as Reagan had predicted they would.

As with any group so large, different people had different experiences. But it's safe to say that legalization did make life better for many of these legalized immigrants. Better jobs. Better educational opportunities. Freedom from the daily worry of being taken into custody by U.S. immigration officials and being forcibly deported back home.

The following year, by executive order, Reagan extended the benefits to the young children of immigrants who went through the legalization process, the 1980s version of today's so-called DACA Dreamers, young people brought to America before their parents had legal status. Reagan's executive order affected 100,000 families. But that wasn't the end of the story of Ronald Reagan's Immigration Reform and Control Act of 1986. Not even close. The impact of that legislation—and the debate over it—would continue for years . . . decades, really. It is still being debated today. And the opinions go in every direction imaginable.

One aspect of the 1986 law was clearly a failure.

Remember the tough-sounding sanctions that were going to keep employers honest and give them a powerful incentive to stop hiring people who were in the country illegally? The sanctions that were ultimately passed had no teeth at all.

To Reagan, the idea that immigrants could remain here legally was a win for those who had come here with the best of intentions, and it was also a win for the country. Working "on the books" meant they would be paying taxes that would help local communities. Employers were supposed to check IDs and attest to their employees' immigration status. Companies were supposed to face severe fines and other penalties for knowingly recruiting or hiring unauthorized workers. But in the fierce negotiations before the bill became law, business groups had managed to limit that provision so much that it was meaningless. Under the amended law, all employers had to do was show they had *tried*. That loophole was so gigantic, almost no one was ever prosecuted. The employers *knew* they wouldn't get in trouble. They had no real incentive to give up the cheap undocumented labor they had grown used to. And with jobs still open north of the border in construction, agriculture, manufacturing, hospitality, roadwork, lawn care, you name it, fresh waves of immigrants kept streaming across.

All that badly undermined one of the key goals of the 1986 immigration reform: to slow those future waves to a trickle.

And so today all those industries and others still rely heavily on undocumented labor. They keep hiring for the same reasons Reagan objected to. The immigrants work hard. They are often paid less. They are slow to complain. And the companies that hire them rarely get busted for it. Clearly, the 1986 reform did not reverse that rough American reality, no matter how good Reagan, Simpson, and Mazzoli's intentions were. And so today we have four times the number of people in the United States illegally as we had in the 1980s . . . and no real prospect of solving the problem as long as Republicans and Democrats remain so divided on the issue. I'd say *more divided* now than ever in modern times.

In the decades that followed, other presidents would seek to overhaul the nation's immigration system, with what can only be called marginal success. President Bush in 1990. President Clinton in 1996. Neither of those efforts was nearly as ambitious or as impactful as Reagan's. President George W. Bush had an ambitious plan for comprehensive immigration reform that echoed some of Reagan's ideas. It would have provided legal status and a path to citizenship for the approximately 12 million undocumented immigrants already in the United States. The bill, which included three hundred miles of border fence and 20,000 more Border Patrol agents, was pitched as a compromise between enforcement and compassion. After heated debate on both sides of the aisle, it went down to defeat in June 2007, never to be revived again.

President Obama talked a big game but never put his personal political capital or his filibuster-proof majority behind the issue. President Trump talked a lot about building a wall across the entire southern border and getting Mexico to pay for it. He built fifty-two miles and didn't collect a single peso in return. President Biden signed a couple of minor executive orders but has never even tried to get a comprehensive immigration plan through Congress. The issue was too toxic, his people said.

Over the years, the issue of immigration would remain front and center in American politics as each party attacked the other. Enforcement efforts would rise and fall. The waves of immigrants would ebb and flow. Politicians from both parties would keep rushing to Texas, New Mexico, Arizona, and California to hold press conferences at the border, denouncing the failures of our immigration system. And no one would get anywhere near another comprehensive reform.

How important was immigration to Ronald Reagan? So important that, of all the topics he could have chosen, he would devote his final speech as president to this one, talking just as passionately and just as personally as he did in the Mondale debate—maybe even more so.

It's a moving speech, worth quoting at some length even now.

"Other countries may seek to compete with us," he said that day. "But in one vital area, as a beacon of freedom and opportunity that draws the people of the world, no country on earth comes close. This, I believe, is one of the most important sources of America's greatness. We lead the world because, unique among nations, we draw our people, our strength, from every country and every corner of the world. And by doing so we continuously renew and enrich our nation."

He quoted from a letter he had recently received.

"'You can go to live in France, but you cannot become a Frenchman,'" the letter said. "'You can go to live in Germany or Turkey or Japan, but you cannot become a German, a Turk, or Japanese. But anyone from any corner of the Earth can come to live in America and become an American.'"

That should be a source of strength for us, Reagan said, not division.

"Yes, the torch of Lady Liberty symbolizes our freedom and represents our heritage, the compact with our parents, our grandparents, and our ancestors. It is that lady who gives us our great and special place in the world. For it's the great life force of each generation of new Americans that guarantees that America's triumph shall continue unsurpassed into the next century and beyond."

That, he said, is what it means to dream the American Dream.

"While other countries cling to the stale past, here in America we breathe life into dreams," he said. "We create the future, and the world follows us into tomorrow. Thanks to each wave of new arrivals to this land of opportunity, we're a nation forever young, forever bursting with energy and new ideas, and always on the cutting edge, always leading the world to the next frontier. This quality is vital to our future as a nation. If we ever closed the door to new Americans, our leadership in the world would soon be lost."

He told the story of an East German who had been a POW in the United States during World War II and recalled with great fondness his time in the American prison camp. The man loved being jailed in America more than he liked being "free" at home in East Germany.

"It is bold men and women, yearning for freedom and opportunity, who leave their homelands and come to a new country to start their lives over. They believe in the American dream. And over and over, they make it come true for themselves, for their children, and for others. They give more than they receive. They labor and succeed. And often they are entrepreneurs. But their greatest contribution is more than economic, because they understand in a special way how glorious it is to be an American. They renew our pride and gratitude in the United States of America, the greatest, freest nation in the world, the last, best hope of man on Earth."

CHAPTER 15

FADING TEFLON

For a long time, nothing ever stuck to Ronald Reagan.
Then senior people in the White House started thinking they might be untouchable, that official policy and
the federal law weren't necessarily meant for them. Bad,
bad idea.

LESSON LEARNED: PERSONNEL IS POLICY.

He really was the "Teflon president."

As the years rolled on, Reagan displayed a remarkable ability
to deflect criticism, project a positive image, and maintain broad
public support. Anything unwelcome just seemed to slide off him,
no matter how bad the news of the moment might be. When the
federal deficit skyrocketed, when the economy tumbled into recession, when the gas tax went up, when the nation's savings and loans
began to falter, Reagan never suffered much politically. Even a
would-be assassin's bullet couldn't slow him down for long.

Much to the frustration of his partisan foes, Reagan's charisma and strong connection to the American people carried him merrily along.

Congresswoman Patricia Schroeder, a liberal Democrat from Colorado, was the one who coined the term. She took to the House floor one day in 1983 to denounce the Republican president for something or other. She said, "He has been perfecting the Teflon-coated presidency. He sees to it that nothing sticks to him." Schroeder later explained that the expression had come to her while she was frying eggs in a nonstick pan.

Well, as any home chef can tell you, Teflon doesn't last forever. It peels off eventually. And so it was with the protective coating on Reagan's presidency. It wasn't nearly strong enough to withstand the Iran-Contra affair.

By the usual standards of twentieth-century America, Reagan had had a remarkably scandal-free administration. But when he finally got ensnared in something genuinely scandalous, it was a real beaut, something he couldn't talk, smile, or charm his way out of. Iran-Contra provoked bipartisan uproar, launched televised congressional hearings, and—once independent counsel Lawrence Walsh got going—delivered federal felony indictments to a wide swath of Reagan's foreign policy team, including Defense Secretary Caspar Weinberger, National Security Advisor Robert McFarlane, replacement National Security Advisor John Poindexter, Assistant Secretary of State Elliott Abrams, national security aide Colonel Oliver North, CIA covert-operations chief Clair George, CIA Central America chief Alan Fiers, and several other key figures.

Though Reagan would never be impeached or criminally charged in the Iran-Contra scandal, he still paid. His poll numbers took a beating. His reputation was stained at home and abroad. And he had to admit on national television that he had deceived the American people when he claimed he'd never traded arms for hostages with the terror-exporting government of Iran.

Yes, a giant mess all around.

Iran-Contra was the absolute low point of the Reagan administration, and it started with arguably good intent. But its impact on Reagan's presidency and Reagan's legacy was undeniable. Would he recover eventually? Would his vision, personality, and policies pull him through? For a while there, it all looked seriously iffy. Certainly, once the Iran-Contra scandal swept in, Reagan was no longer gliding through the presidency as he had in the past.

So, what if anything did Reagan learn from that painful experience? What can we learn from the way he, his top aides, and the assorted probers and investigators handled the fallout? Three and a half decades later, those questions matter even more than the particular policy clashes at the center of it all. At its core though, Iran-Contra proved a truism that every president learns either the easy way or the hard way: personnel *is* policy.

The roots of the scandal go back to the hostage crisis in Iran at the end of the Carter administration and to Reagan's long-standing commitment to anti-communism.

When the fifty-two Americans were released just as Reagan was coming into office, he continued Carter's ban on weapons sales to the hostage-taking government of Iran. Ayatollah Ruhollah Khomeini was vowing to export his Islamic revolution across the

Middle East. His militant regime was funding and supporting the spread of international terrorism. Reagan lined up with Carter on this one: he declared that the United States had no business selling arms to these violent, anti-American zealots.

Some senior officials in the Reagan administration saw the embargo as pointless. The Iranians could easily purchase military hardware from other sources, they argued. Wasn't the American embargo only pushing Iran toward the Soviet Union? If the United States resumed arms sales to Iran, these administration officials contended, maybe moderate factions in the Khomeini government would pressure the Islamic paramilitary group Hezbollah to free seven American hostages then being held in Lebanon. *Arms for hostages*—that was the expression being tossed around. Now at war with Iraq, Iran was desperate for TOW anti-tank missiles, Hawk antiaircraft missiles, and other American weaponry.

At the same time, right-wing rebels in Honduras were waging a guerrilla war to overthrow the leftist Sandinista government in Nicaragua. Since the day he took office, Reagan had been eager to help the contras, as the fighters were known. That desire raised a clear alarm in Congress, which passed the Boland Amendment, banning all such aid. Instead of following the law and official U.S. policy, senior White House officials set up a secret scheme they code-named "the Enterprise." High-tech weapons were sold illegally through Israel to Iran. The CIA then funneled millions of dollars in profits, also illegally, to the anti-Nicaraguan rebels while also helping to recruit, train, and arm them. To justify that part of the equation, the administration relied in part on a secret 1984 order from Reagan directing the National Security Council to "keep the Contras together 'body and soul,'" directly contradicting what Congress had voted for.

There was no way this was ever going to stay secret. It was a massive operation involving the Defense Department, the State Department, as well as the National Security Council, the CIA, and assorted other federal agencies. The leak appeared first in a Lebanese magazine citing a knowledgeable Iranian source just after the U.S. midterm elections in November of 1986. Suddenly the story was everywhere. The Democrats in Congress went berserk. Questions were flying in all directions, the most incendiary of them being these two:

What did Reagan know? And what did Reagan *do*?

The follow-ups were just as predictable: Had he ordered the illegal arms-for-hostages swap with Iran? Did he know that the proceeds were being sent to the contras? Or was all this occurring in the White House without the president's knowledge or consent? Whatever the answers, this much was certain: none of it would make Reagan look good. The entire Enterprise was illegal *and* profoundly dumb. Either Reagan was involved, or he was so disengaged from the daily operations of the White House that he had no idea what was happening right under his nose. Involved or clueless? Take your pick. Both choices stunk. So Reagan went with option number three.

He bobbed and weaved.

On November 13, he addressed the country from the Oval Office without ever quite saying which it was. He tried to explain, tried to defend—and what came out was more like a cloudy stew. "My purpose was . . . to send a signal that the United States was prepared to replace the animosity between [the U.S. and Iran] with a new relationship. . . . At the same time we undertook this initiative, we made clear that Iran must oppose all forms of international terrorism as a condition of progress in our relationship. The most significant step which Iran could take, we indicated, would be to use its influence in Lebanon to secure the release of all hostages held there."

Huh?

His efforts to calm the roiling waters were not working. Politically, he began to take a beating, something he hadn't really experienced before. His sky-high 67-percent approval rating was suddenly at a far more down-to-earth 46 percent, according to a *New York Times*/CBS poll—"the largest single drop for any U.S. president in history," the pollsters said. Where was the Teflon now? And things only got worse later that month when news broke that Lieutenant Colonel Oliver North, a senior aide on the National Security Council, illegally destroyed documents revealing details of the plan, and that North's boss, National Security Advisor John Poindexter, shred the only signed copy of the presidential order authorizing the missile shipments to Iran. Two days before Thanksgiving, Reagan fired North and accepted Poindexter's resignation.

That same day, Reagan did what politicians often do when they want to buy themselves some time. He appointed a commission, putting John Tower, a former Republican senator from Texas, in charge. Unfortunately for Reagan, the Tower Commission got right to work, interviewing nearly eighty witnesses, including Reagan, who appeared on December 2.

His answers were still hard to follow. When asked about his

WHAT WOULD REAGAN DO?

role in authorizing the arms-to-Iran deal, he seemed to say he had. Then he contradicted himself, saying he didn't remember approving anything like that. That quickly morphed into a firmer denial. It was an unsatisfying performance all around, and it did little to calm the uproar. By the end of the day, whatever Reagan was saying about Iran-Contra, no one was buying anymore. Then, for three long months—an eternity in politics—as the story continued swirling and new details kept trickling in, Reagan stayed mum.

The White House released no detailed statements. The president held no Iran-Contra press conferences. When ABC's Sam Donaldson and the other White House reporters shouted questions beneath the whirring blades of Marine One, Reagan didn't hear—or pretended not to.

At times like these, silence almost always makes things worse. It gives oxygen to the most damaging interpretations, even the crazy ones. It makes people wonder: If you did nothing wrong, why hide? If you did something wrong, why aren't you confronting it, explaining what you did and why? Where was the plainspoken, tell-it-like-it-is Ronald Reagan? As 1986 gave way to 1987, that guy was nowhere to be found. As a result, the damage to Reagan's presidency festered and grew. And the questions got even darker. They included: Given all this, would Reagan be able to achieve anything in the second half of his second term?

When the Tower Commission report came out on February 26—lightning speed for Washington—it laid out the whole nefarious Enterprise, making clear that the Reagan administration *did* seek to trade arms for hostages. The report slammed Oliver North, John Poindexter, Caspar Weinberger, and a host of other administration officials for violating U.S. policy and U.S. law. The commission concluded that Reagan probably knew about some of this, but he was most likely unaware of the extent of the arms-for-hostages deal and the diversion of money and weapons to the contras.

His biggest sin, according to the Tower Commission, was failing to supervise his subordinates and being insufficiently aware of their actions. It was about as good as the president could have hoped for, though it didn't come close to making the controversy go away. Finally, on March 4, he sat before the TV cameras again and tried to explain. Clearly, all this had taken a toll on him. He still looked like the Reagan of old. But he sounded shaken, uncharacteristically unsure of himself. At least he was *trying* to confront the issue head-on.

Said Reagan: "The reason I haven't spoken to you before now is this: You deserve the truth. And as frustrating as the waiting has been, I felt it was improper to come to you with sketchy reports or possibly even erroneous statements, which would then have to be corrected, creating even more doubt and confusion. There's been enough of that." But after briefly tipping his hat to the acceptance of "full responsibility," Reagan made clear he was blaming his aides. "I take full responsibility for my own actions and for those of my administration. As angry as I may be about activities undertaken without my knowledge, I am still accountable for those activities. As disappointed as I may be in some who served me, I'm still the one who must answer to the American people for this behavior."

He did back down a bit from one of his previous denials. "A few months ago," he allowed, "I told the American people I did not trade arms for hostages. My heart and my best intentions still tell me that's true, but the facts and the evidence tell me it is not." That was the admission. Next came the attempted explanation: "As the Tower board reported, what began as a strategic opening to Iran deteriorated, in its implementation, into trading arms for hostages. This runs counter to my own beliefs, to administration policy, and to the original strategy we had in mind."

He still denied that he had known anything about the diversion of money and weapons to his beloved contras. But Reagan's comments were the furthest he'd come so far. Still, they left considerable doubt about his own role. Had he known about the two-part scheme? Did he approve it? Among those who had their own strong feelings on that were the very aides who partly took the fall for him, as several of them made clear in the books they later wrote about the Iran-Contra affair. "Ronald Reagan knew of and approved a great deal of what went on with both the Iranian initiative and private efforts on behalf of the Contras and he received regular, detailed briefings on both," Oliver North said in *Under Fire: An American Story*. North was unequivocal: "I have no doubt that he was told about the use of residuals for the Contras, and that he approved it. Enthusiastically."

The earlier, handwritten notes of Caspar Weinberger said much the same thing, offering his own theory about why Reagan felt justified in breaking the law. "He could answer charges of illegality but he couldn't answer the charge that 'big strong President Reagan passed up a chance to free hostages,'" the then defense secretary wrote to himself on December 7, 1985.

The investigations and analyses would continue. For years. That

November, the Democratic-controlled Congress issued a report saying the Reagan administration was guilty of "secrecy, deception and disdain for the law. . . . If the president did not know what his national security advisers were doing, he should have." So, what did Reagan know? "On this critical point," the report concluded, "the shredding of documents by Poindexter, North and others, and the death of [CIA director William] Casey, leave the record incomplete."

And the stench of the scandal stayed around for a very long time.

As for all those senior officials who were swept up in the various probes, many of them were prosecuted by independent counsel Lawrence Walsh. Six—Robert McFarlane, John Poindexter, Elliott Abrams, Oliver North, Alan Fiers, and Clair George—either pleaded guilty or were found guilty after jury trials. The charges included perjury, obstruction of justice, withholding evidence, and destroying documents. Also convicted were several former military and intelligence officials who helped execute the Enterprise and an Iranian-American businessman who laundered the illegal funds. Two of North's closest aides, his secretary Fawn Hall and his liaison Jonathan Scott Royster, were given immunity from prosecution in exchange for testifying against him.

There hadn't ever been a White House perp walk quite the size of this one—not that anybody could recall. But that didn't mean the federal prisons needed to make extra room for Iran-Contra felons. None of the main players ever did a day behind bars. North and Poindexter had their convictions overturned on appeal. And on Christmas Eve of 1992, after he'd been defeated for reelection,

President George H. W. Bush, who of course had been Reagan's vice president, pardoned Abrams, McFarlane, Fiers, George, and also Caspar Weinberger, whose case hadn't yet come to trial.

There's one great thing, maybe *only* one, about terrible messes: they are valuable learning opportunities . . . for those whose minds are open enough. And it's often easier to grasp the lessons in hindsight.

So, what did Reagan learn from the Iran-Contra debacle? And what can *we* learn now? Thankfully, we've had plenty of time to absorb and digest. For one thing, yes, it was a true debacle, the single worst chapter of Reagan's two extraordinary terms. That truth hasn't faded in the decades since. Iran-Contra and Reagan's reaction to it didn't just deflate his poll numbers and damage him politically. The scandal also undermined America's moral standing around the world. Suddenly, it became a whole lot harder for U.S. officials to lecture other nations on the dangers of giving concessions to hostage takers and the importance of the rule of law.

Reagan's openness to negotiating with Iran and Hezbollah were almost certainly well motivated, as he insisted they were. But they also may well have planted dangerous ideas in the minds of America's enemies. It certainly gave the bad guys an easy excuse, signaling that hostage taking might be a useful way to extract political and financial concessions from us. In the years that followed, that was a tool some rogue nations repeatedly tried to use to their own advantage.

So the first real lesson has to be: Don't do that. Tempting as it might sometimes be to conduct business with international extortionists, it's rarely a good long-term play. Same with illegally delivering arms and money to foreign guerrilla groups in violation of U.S. law. Even if you are sympathetic to their cause, no one in America is above the law, including presidents. And thanks to the media, to law enforcement, and to the deeply ingrained "gotcha" culture of Washington, White House lawbreakers usually get caught. From Teapot Dome to Watergate to Iran-Contra, America in the twentieth century was loaded with instructive examples—just like the twenty-first century is turning out to be.

Reagan seemed to learn that lesson. The proof? He never found himself in a position like this again.

Another important lesson he learned and so can we: when you find yourself in trouble, silence is often your enemy. Deceiving and obfuscating are even bigger enemies. And your biggest enemy of all? Changing your story as you go along. As the contradictions pile up, people start asking: Why should we believe *anything* you say? And they have a point. When two stories collide directly, both of them can't be true.

Reagan's shifting explanations for Iran-Contra put him in an impossible jam and handed his opponents a giant rhetorical club to beat him with. Was the president involved . . . or clueless? Was his memory so poor that he couldn't remember? Was he lying then . . . or was he lying now? If these are the questions flying at you, no answer is sufficient. You've already lost. But Reagan being Reagan, he also set some positive examples during Iran-Contra, some things he did right that are worth copying even now.

Stick to the values you believe in. Fire people who need to be fired. Reagan did plenty of that, starting with Oliver North. The president was ill-served by key White House staffers, even if they thought they were doing his bidding. They had to go. Once the damage was done, they needed to move on. Reagan continued with some new faces around him and some big goals ahead. But the biggest lesson he teaches this time, as always, was to take responsibility for the mistakes and then simply persevere. As the walls closed in around him, he had every reason to feel disappointed, to feel shamed, to feel depressed about the controversy and the toll it was taking on him. At times, he may well have felt some of that, though given the short leash he allowed those kinds of emotions, with Reagan it was always hard to tell.

But this much is clear: He kept pressing on. He got back to business. He stayed focused on the job. He launched fresh initiatives.

Eventually, the Iran-Contra story slipped from the front pages. His poll numbers even bounced back. And he didn't let the questions about his future lead to paralysis. He was still Ronald Reagan. Some of the Teflon even returned for him. He had a lot left to achieve.

CHAPTER 16

FIRST FRIEND

She was his superpower, his sounding board, and his not-so-secret weapon all rolled into one. She was there for him in ways that no one else ever managed to be. He had no idea what he would do without her.

LESSON LEARNED: LIFE'S A WHOLE LOT
EASIER WHEN YOU HAVE THE RIGHT PARTNER
WATCHING YOUR BACK—ALWAYS.

You really can't explain Ronald Reagan without explaining Nancy and the profound role she played in the final four decades of his life. So I won't even try. In Jane Wyman, he'd chosen someone who later turned out to be the *wrong* person. In Nancy, he felt tremendously blessed to have found the right one. In many ways, his second marriage was the more traditional of the two, defined by the familiar values of mid-twentieth-century America. She subsumed her career into his. She looked after their children and their homes. As a young woman in Hollywood, finding a husband had been her number one priority ... and then she found the right one in the president's office at the Screen Actors Guild.

"I was never really a career woman," she explained years later, saying she went to work "only because I hadn't found the man I wanted to marry. I couldn't sit around and do nothing, so I became an actress." When he got her name removed from the notorious McCarthy-era Hollywood blacklist, she was grateful she could work again as an MGM contract player and grateful to the union president who had cleared up the misunderstanding. They stayed in touch, as they promised they would. They dated, while they both dated others. Still gun-shy after his divorce, Reagan wasn't eager to rush back to the altar. His two children with Jane, Maureen and Michael, were still in elementary school, and Jane's acting career was still thriving. But he enjoyed Nancy's easy company. He welcomed her soothing nature and her laser focus on him, and he especially welcomed the prospect of greater domestic stability. They tied the knot on March 4, 1952, in a thoroughly low-key ceremony at Studio City's Little Brown Church. William Holden and his actress wife, Brenda Marshall, were the best man and matron of honor ... and the only guests. After the short ceremony, the four of them went back to the Holdens' house for dinner and cake. The newlyweds honeymooned in Arizona, and a whole new adventure began. Daughter Patti was born in October 1952. While Reagan stayed active in the union for the rest of the decade, alternating as president and board member, he and Nancy appeared together in 1957's *Hellcats of the Navy*. But after their son Ron (Ronald Prescott Reagan Jr.) was born the following year, she became a full-time wife and mother, and that was it for Nancy's acting career.

But hold on a second here. . . .

Despite the many marital milestones, it's a huge mistake to write off Nancy Reagan as a throwback from an earlier day, a happy helpmate merely along for the ride as her husband soared to the governor's mansion in Sacramento and all the way to the White House. That overlooks too much: her steely willpower, her own political savvy, her quiet persistence, and her unwavering commitment to protecting her husband—*no matter what!*—and also getting her way. She left the spotlight mostly to him. And focused as she was on her husband, she wasn't always the easiest mom or stepmom, as her children all made clear over the years in their books and interviews. But as a dedicated wife, a world-class confidence builder, and a steadfast life partner, Nancy Reagan was in a category all by herself. She was a dogged promoter and protector of her husband's well-being. To the repeated chagrin of some sharp-elbowed political insiders who made the mistake of crossing her, she was also a legendarily ruthless string puller around the White House.

Just ask Donald Regan.

He was the second-most-powerful person at 1600 Pennsylvania Avenue until, one day in early 1987, he managed to offend the First Lady. The next thing he knew, he was packing his boxes and changing his TV chyron to "*former* White House chief of staff."

The breaking point between the two of them? Nancy's personal astrologer. The chief of staff didn't think the First Lady should have a personal astrologer sharing insights from the stars (and not the Hollywood kind) about trip dates, bill drafts, and policy positions. "Virtually every major move and decision the Reagans made during my time as White House Chief of Staff was cleared in advance with a woman in San Francisco who drew up horoscopes to make certain that the planets were in a favorable alignment for the enterprise," Regan grumbled in his memoir, *For the Record*. Nancy didn't appreciate the meddling, said so to her husband, and the chief of staff—not the astrologer and certainly not the First Lady—was gone, *just like that*, replaced by former Senate majority leader Howard Baker, who never made the mistake of complaining about Nancy's astrologer or much of anything else.

She was famous for "the gaze," the adoring, almost unblinking way she looked at the man she almost always called "Ronnie." She was "Mommie" to him, and for both of them, the lovey-dovey stuff never ceased, right down to the endless stream of love letters he wrote to her across the decades. In one "Dear Wife" letter, chosen more or less at random, he declares: "Whatever I treasure and enjoy—this home, our ranch, the sight of the sea—all would be without meaning if I didn't have you. I live in a permanent Christmas because God gave me you."

When he was in the hospital recuperating from the 1981 assassination attempt, Nancy wrote in her diary: "Nothing can happen to my Ronnie. My life would be over." So, yes, it was also a mutual thing, even though her public persona was far less gushy than his.

While the president projected a warm and folksy and down-to-earth image—"someone you'd want to have a beer with," as commentators felt almost compelled to say—no one ever described the First Lady that way. This isn't to say she lacked social skills. Her friends all found her bright and perky and caring. In public settings, she'd certainly mastered "charm-and-disarm" persuasion, even if it was backed by a certain rumored ruthlessness. But she was undeniably pricklier and more rigid than her husband. To those inclined to criticize—a crowded category that included millions of Democrats, media, liberal Hollywood types, and, yes, her children—she could seem imperious and self-absorbed and to lack a common touch.

For years she made headlines for all the wrong reasons, dinged for spending extravagantly on clothing, home decorating, and other flashy purchases. It's true she didn't always have a good instinct for the impression she left with the public. Ordering a large collection of expensive china for the White House in the depths of the recession—she might have thought twice about that, even though the purchase was privately funded. Soon she was being pilloried by newspaper editorial cartoonists as a latter-day Marie Antoinette and parodied in a recurring sketch on *Saturday Night Live*, played in drag by Terry Sweeney, the show's first openly gay cast member.

But you know who didn't seem to notice any of Nancy's alleged foibles—or care about them if he did? You know who found her infinitely charming and delightful day after day, year after year? Her husband, who loved her just the way she was, and that never faded. And he never got tired of saying so. She largely embraced his view of politics and the world . . . or came around eventually. And he seemed convinced that, in many ways, she really did know what was best for him.

They enjoyed each other's company and that of couples who were their longtime friends. The closest tended to be wealthy Californians, people they'd first gotten to know in the General Electric days or from the showbiz world. Many had ties to Palm Springs, that favorite haunt of West Coast business titans and Old Hollywood. The group partly overlapped with the president's "kitchen cabinet." These close pals included Walter and Leonore Annenberg. (The Reagans spent many a New Year's Eve at the Annenbergs' two-hundred-acre Sunnylands estate in Rancho Mirage, where the other guests might include Dean Martin, Bing Crosby, Sammy Davis Jr., Lucille Ball, Bob Hope, Los Angeles Dodgers Hall of Fame pitcher Don Sutton, or, in later years, Gerald and Betty Ford.) Also at the top of the friends' list were Alfred and Betsy Bloomingdale. (Philanthropist and socialite Betsy, who made the best-dressed lists and supposedly had eleven closets in the couple's Holmby Hills home, was often described as "Nancy's best friend.") Frequently in the mix were Frank and Barbara Sinatra. (When the president was shot in 1981, it was Frank who flew immediately to Washington to be at Nancy's service.) And don't forget fashion designer James Galanos. (Nancy's collection of Galanos dresses included the white-beaded, one-shoulder, lace-over-silk satin gown she wore for the 1981 inaugural. "Nobody could afford to dress completely with Jimmy," she said, signifying frugality on the Nancy curve. "I hang on to what I have.")

Old friend Charlton Heston called the Reagan marriage "probably the greatest love affair in the history of the American Presidency." But the plain fact of the matter was that, with Nancy, there was always a lot more going on, a whole lot more than most people realized. As Jimmy Stewart supposedly said: "If Ronald Reagan had married Nancy the first time around, she could have got him an Academy Award." Whether that was true or not, Reagan seemed to believe it.

Nancy was smarter than most people gave her credit for—and far more politically canny, sometimes more than the veteran consultants, strategists, and aides who hovered around her husband. She never upstaged "Ronnie." But her influence was profound, far beyond her push on the issue of illegal drugs, the one contribution most people remember. She softened his sharper edges. Urged him to be more pragmatic and encouraged his relationship with Tip O'Neill. At budget time, she worked to preserve programs that aided the poor. And when her husband spoke out strongly against abortion, she urged him not to go out too far on that political limb, reminding him that most Americans weren't as staunchly right-to-life as the ardent activists were. She encouraged tolerance toward people of all sexual persuasions at a time when gay rights was nowhere on the Republican agenda, inviting several gay friends from Hollywood to the White House. And she certainly encouraged her husband's meetings with Mikhail Gorbachev.

Veteran Washington correspondent Owen Ullmann noted that he'd certainly filed his share of negative Nancy stories. But he said he'd changed his view of her after covering the White House for *USA Today.* "I came to appreciate the enormous influence Nancy Reagan had on her husband's domestic and foreign policies to ensure a successful presidency," Ullmann wrote. "She was his only close confidant and friend, and his No. 1 adviser. In retrospect, I must say she served him—and the country—very well."

After all, no one knew him as well as she did, and no one was quite as dedicated. Sometimes that meant she worried more. As the 1984 reelection campaign kicked into high gear, most of the political pros figured Reagan had it in the bag against Walter Mondale as long as the Democrat focused his attacks on Star Wars and the president's supposed indifference to the needs of the poor. That stuff would never connect with voters, the pros were sure. That was probably true. But in their overblown confidence, some of them also tried to explain away Reagan's disastrous performance in the first debate, chalking it up to a "bad night" or being rusty from the isolation of the White House. Full speed ahead, they said.

Nancy knew better. She had no illusions. That bad night was no fluke, she believed. She and a small handful of her husband's very closest advisors—James Baker, Michael Deaver, Stuart Spencer— had been growing concerned by what they saw as a certain lack of focus on Reagan's part and a decline in his mental dexterity. As the *Washington Post*'s longtime Reagan watcher Lou Cannon put it in his excellent biography, *President Reagan: The Role of a Lifetime*, "They viewed the conservative pleas to 'let Reagan be Reagan' as an invitation to catastrophe and, almost without discussion, reached an early command decision that there would be no news conferences during the fall reelection campaign. (Reagan's last formal news conference before the election was on July 24, five days after Mondale was nominated.)"

There was no intervention. There was no come-to-Jesus moment. There was just a quiet agreement between Nancy and the inner-inner circle, those who knew Reagan best: *We can't have him hanging out there in a lot of unscripted situations. This is a time for discipline, protection, and control.*

Following that approach, Reagan sailed to a second term with a history-making win.

There are those who believe that Nancy's protective instinct might have given her husband another four years. There's no way to prove that one way or the other. But this much was clear: he didn't fight her diagnosis or her prescription. Gratefully, he listened when she spoke up for him.

Most presidential spouses (only First *Ladies* . . . so far) manage to find a cause, something they can get their hearts around, a charitable focus or two that comes to define their time in the White House. If they are lucky and they work hard enough, they'll have the satisfaction of actually helping to ease a national crisis and make life better for some group of needy Americans.

No matter who's elected, there's never any shortage of need.

Being married to the president has always been a powerful platform, and it might as well be used for good. No one needed to explain any of that to Nancy Reagan. She'd been in public life long enough. She understood this role instinctively. For her, it was really just a matter of figuring out what to focus on, how to leverage her public platform most effectively, and how best to get her husband involved.

She tried on a few options.

She made time to visit military veterans, old folks, and disabled people. She appeared at events to promote the Foster Grandparents Program, a terrific network that connects over-fifty-five volunteers with at-risk children. But it was her work on the issue of drug abuse—drug abuse by young people, especially—that she became best known for and where she had her greatest impact.

If Nancy Reagan's time as First Lady had its own slogan, it would have to be her three-word admonition to teenagers who faced peer pressure to start using drugs.

"Just Say No."

The phrase, which she almost single-handedly popularized, has been a touchstone and a lightning rod in many discussions about drug use, drug policy, and the nation's so-called War on Drugs. But those three words remain a beacon of clarity and a goal worth striving for, even today.

She got to the issue early, during the 1980 campaign, when she made a stop at Daytop Village, a residential drug treatment program in New York City known for its demanding, tough-love philosophy. In those days, drug treatment programs were not usually on the Republican presidential campaign schedule. Too many politicians from both parties like to condemn drug use, demand that "something be done," and leave it at that, never bothering to meet a single peer counselor, program administrator, or struggling drug addict. Meanwhile, marijuana was everywhere. So were cocaine, heroin, and misused prescription pills. Fentanyl wasn't here yet, but methamphetamines were taking hold, and highly addictive crack cocaine would soon be on the way.

Daytop was a gritty place, run by a charismatic Catholic monsignor named William O'Brien, where the young clients were expected to display rugged honesty as they faced themselves, their addictions, and their own recoveries. Prior to my time as governor, I served on the board of Daytop's New Jersey chapter. It was there I learned about addiction as a disease and got the knowledge and compassion to advocate for more treatment as governor and to chair Donald Trump's Opioid Commission. Daytop didn't work for everyone, but miracles were happening there every day and in other drug treatment programs across America.

Nancy was moved.

Her own children were past the entry-ramp, young-teenage years. Her youngest, Ron, was twenty-two, busy pursuing his life-long dream of dancing with the Joffrey Ballet. But as a mother, she'd done her share of worrying, and she knew that countless millions of young Americans were being pulled in dangerous directions. Young people, she believed, needed practical tools and moral support if they were going to sidestep deadly mistakes. And no one, regardless of age, geography, economic status, or family support, was ever fully immune. Addicts were everywhere.

After the Reagans got to the White House, the First Lady returned to Daytop and vowed to help. The best way, she concluded, was to promote public awareness and use her powerful platform as First Lady to highlight the real-life dangers of drugs. "Understanding what drugs can do to your children, understanding peer pressure and understanding why they turn to drugs," she said, that's "the first step in solving the problem."

The famous phrase came from a stop at Longfellow Elementary School in Oakland, California, where a girl had a question for the visiting First Lady: What should she do if she was offered drugs by a friend?

"You just say 'no,'" the president's wife told the student. And so a seed was planted. The following year, a New York advertising agency, Needham, Harper & Steers/USA, built a multimedia campaign around the slogan, aimed explicitly at twelve- to fourteen-year-olds. But it was Nancy Reagan who slipped the concept into the American bloodstream and opened a new front—pop culture—in the War on Drugs. Though some critics derided the campaign as simple-minded, Just Say No student groups were soon popping up in schools across the country. Preteens were making no-drug pledges with their friends. It wasn't much longer until the airwaves were deluged with Just Say No public service announcements from the National Institute on Drug Abuse featuring saxophone-playing and breakdancing teens, looking healthy and having fun without the need for chemical enhancement. Michael Jackson recorded a "Just Say No" version of "Beat It" that aired on *The Flintstone Kids*. And Nancy kept touring to promote the stay-clean cause. Visiting schools and drug programs. Writing op-ed pieces and sitting for dozens of media interviews. By 1985, she'd promoted the cause on two dozen talk shows, co-hosted a segment on ABC's *Good Morning America*, starred in a two-hour PBS documentary, and appeared as herself in an episode of the sitcom *Diff'rent Strokes*. How's that for taking it to the people? During her husband's second term, she expanded the campaign internationally, inviting the presidential spouses of thirty nations to the White House for the "First Ladies Conference on Drug Abuse." She later became the first American First Lady to address the United Nations.

Nancy meant business.

Meanwhile, at her gentle but persistent urging, her husband was reprioritizing the nation's War on Drugs, which was first declared by Richard Nixon in the early 1970s. President Reagan signed the Anti-Drug Abuse Act of 1986, which budgeted $1.7 billion in fresh funding and established mandatory minimum prison sentences for certain drug offenses. Most people today think the stiff sentences went too far, expecting the criminal-justice system to solve problems that also required heavy applications of education, treatment, medicine, community support, parental involvement, and mental health care. But no one has ever questioned the need for public education as part of any well-rounded anti-drug campaign.

And Nancy kept at it.

So, did "Just Say No" work? Yes, actually, there's evidence that it did, if by *work* we mean increasing public awareness, convincing some young people not to start using drugs, and pulling her husband into the fight. It's always hard to establish direct correlations on an issue as complex as this one. But credible surveys from the era showed a sharp spike in public concern over the country's drug issues. In 1985, the proportion of Americans who saw drug abuse as the nation's "number one problem" was between 2 percent and 6 percent. By 1989, that number had jumped to 64 percent. "Just Say No" played an undeniable role in advancing that.

At the same time, the National Institute on Drug Abuse survey of adolescent attitudes also showed some progress during the Reagan years. Progress among kids who were already using. More progress for those who were at risk of getting started. One study found that marijuana use among high school seniors slipped from 33 percent in 1980 to 12 percent in 1991. Be skeptical of drug use statistics if you want to. But the First Lady wasn't driven by statistics. That wasn't the point.

"If you can save just one child, it's worth it," she said.

Never was that commitment clearer—by both of them—than in the President's Address to the Nation on September 14, 1986. In a sharp break with protocol, Nancy joined him that night.

"Good evening," the president said. "Usually, I talk with you from my office in the West Wing of the White House. But tonight there's something special to talk about, and I've asked someone very special to join me. Nancy and I are here in the West Hall of the White House, and around us are the rooms in which we live. It's the home you've provided for us, of which we merely have temporary custody."

A very Reagan open. Setting the stage gently.

"Nancy's joining me because the message this evening is not my message but ours. And we speak to you not simply as fellow citizens but as fellow parents and grandparents and as concerned neighbors. It's back-to-school time for America's children. And while drug and alcohol abuse cuts across all generations, it's especially damaging to the young people on whom our future depends. So tonight, from our family to yours, from our home to yours, thank you for joining us.

"America has accomplished so much in these last few years, whether it's been rebuilding our economy or serving the cause of freedom in the world. What we've been able to achieve has been done with your help—with us working together as a nation united. Now, we need your support again. Drugs are menacing our society. They're threatening our values and undercutting our institutions. They're killing our children."

That was Nancy's cue. "As a mother, I've always thought of September as a special month, a time when we bundled our children off to school, to the warmth of an environment in which they could fulfill the promise and hope in those restless minds. But so much has happened over these last years, so much to shake the foundations of all that we know and all that we believe in. Today there's a drug and alcohol abuse epidemic in this country, and no one is safe from it—not you, not me, and certainly not our children, because this epidemic has their names written on it. Many of you may be thinking: 'Well, drugs don't concern me'—but it does concern you. It concerns us all because of the way it tears at our lives and because it's aimed at destroying the brightness and life of the sons and daughters of the United States."

He picked it up there. "As we mobilize for this national crusade, I'm mindful that drugs are a constant temptation for millions. Please remember this when your courage is tested: You are Americans. You're the product of the freest society mankind has ever known. No one, ever, has the right to destroy your dreams and shatter your life."

"Now," she said in conclusion, "we go on to the next stop: making a final commitment not to tolerate drugs by anyone, anytime, anyplace. So, won't you join us in this great, new national crusade?"

It's hard to know exactly what impact those words might have had on the world. But I think it's fair to say that none of them would have been spoken if Nancy hadn't been there. And whatever the issue, they made one heck of a team.

There are many ways to describe the partnership these two shared. But the clearest one may have come from the presidential historian David Herbert Donald. Asked what single asset a president needs most, he thought for a second and said: "A friend." Throughout their entire marriage, especially their years together in the White House, she was his true and only best friend. A real confidante. Someone obsessively devoted to his best interest. Watching his back and also offering a more objective view. Sharing his dreams and fears as much as his triumphs.

No one could doubt their love or affection. But it was in that role as his friend and protector that Nancy was her husband's biggest asset. It can't be measured in the policy influence she had, though she had plenty. It can't be measured in the fear and respect she instilled in the White House staff, though there was plenty of that. It can't even be measured in the size of the hammer she swung—a large one. No one needs a friend more than a president.

She was truly his first friend.

CHAPTER 17

TEAR DOWN

Worlds can be divided in many ways. By ideas. By civilizations. Even by walls. Committed to ending the Cold War, Reagan went right at its most physical manifestation, the Berlin Wall. If he could get Mr. Gorbachev to "tear down this wall," how much longer till the Cold War was history too?

LESSON LEARNED:
PICK THE BIGGEST TARGET ... AND GO RIGHT FOR IT.

Nothing said "Cold War" quite like the Berlin Wall.

The historic German capital, a bustling city of 3.3 million people, had been divided since right after World War II, the eastern half adhering to Soviet-style communism, the western sector more of a European- or American-style democracy. By 1961, this was becoming a problem for East Germany's communist president, Walter Ulbricht, and his jumpy patron back in Moscow, Soviet leader Nikita Khrushchev. East German citizens, many thousands a month, kept streaming across the border to the West, eager for the freedoms and opportunities they were sorely missing at home. Emboldened by the successes of the Sputnik space program and embarrassed by the steady stream of refugees, including many university students and young professionals, Ulbricht and Khrushchev made their move that August.

They threw up a wall.

According to the two communist leaders, the imposing barrier of concrete blocks and barbed wire was an "antifascist bulwark," needed to keep dangerous westerners from streaming across the border and undermining the socialist state. The true objective was exactly the opposite: to stem the mass defections from east to west.

The wall worked to that extent. The deluge slowed to a trickle. East Berliners remained under the yoke of Soviet oppression. And the people of East Berlin, like those in the rest of communist East Germany, fell further and further behind. The wall remained a practical barrier and a potent symbol—not just of a city divided but also of a world divided, communist from capitalist, darkness from light, the iron fist of oppression from the fresh air of freedom.

Ronald Reagan knew all that . . . and hated it.

Ever since he got to the White House, he'd been eager to put an end to the Cold War, which seemed to have become an almost permanent state of affairs. Never exploding into an all-out shooting war between the two superpowers . . . but never ending, either. The long-running conflict wasn't just an expensive drain on the resources of the United States and the Soviet Union. It wasn't just an excuse for Soviet domination of Eastern Europe. The Cold War also kept igniting in hot spots around the world (Afghanistan, Nicaragua,

Ethiopia, Somalia . . .) while propelling a nuclear arms race that put the future of the entire planet at risk.

But the Cold War was a stubborn beast. It had so many tentacles by the 1980s, it was very difficult to tame. If Reagan needed more proof, all he had to do was glance again at the Iran-Contra affair. The contra part, where the United States hoped to overthrow the Soviet-backed government in Nicaragua, was textbook Cold War. And the Cold War figured into the Iran part of the scandal, too: a big reason Reagan's aides wanted to sell weapons to the terror-spreading *mullahs* in Tehran was the fear that, if the Americans didn't, the Soviets surely would.

Yes, the Cold War cast a shadow over almost *everything*. But for Reagan, finding a way to end it was proving to be a highly elusive goal.

He tried trash talk, declaring the Soviet Union an "Evil Empire." He went searching for someone he could negotiate with, only to be stymied by the Soviet leaders' fragile health and advancing age. Brezhnev was old and tired by the time Reagan took office. The creaky Andropov and even creakier Chernenko came and went too quickly to make any impact at all. It was only when the reform-minded Mikhail Gorbachev rose to power in March of 1985, two months into Reagan's second term, that the American president had a Soviet counterpart who wasn't about to die on him. Reagan knew that eventually America would have to *win* the Cold War— outright win it. But that didn't mean the world couldn't be made safer in the meantime.

And so the superpower summits began. Reagan and Gorbachev

met in Geneva. They met again in Reykjavík. But those high-level sit-downs didn't produce much in the way of concrete results. The two leaders got to know each other, which was good. They took careful measures of each other's temperaments, which was probably necessary. But when it came to reaching any formal, bilateral agreements, they came up woefully short. The most they could agree on was to keep talking, next in Washington and in Moscow after that.

As Reagan grew increasingly impatient, he went looking for other ways to hurry things along. It was only natural that at some point his attention would turn to that potent symbol of Cold War divisions, that jarring physical barrier that literally separated east from west, that frontal assault on the natural unity of the great German capital.

The Berlin Wall.

June 12, 1987. Reagan was due in West Berlin, the free part of the German capital, to help celebrate the 750th anniversary of the city's founding. It wasn't his first time in Berlin or even the first time he had reason to talk about the wall. He'd been there five years earlier, in June of 1982, when he stated, "I'd like to ask the Soviet leaders one question. . . . Why is the wall there?" He'd also addressed the subject in 1986, when the German newspaper *Bild-Zeitung* interviewed him on the wall's twenty-fifth anniversary. "I call upon those responsible to dismantle it," he said that time. The wall was clearly something that had gotten under Reagan's skin. But none of his verbal jabs were having much impact. It was as if no one on the other side was listening. Maybe no one was. But this time, after the previous two summits, he had a personal connection with the leader of the Soviet Union.

Would someone be listening now?

Some of Reagan's advisors urged caution. There was no point in inflaming tensions with the Soviets, they said, not when the two leaders would likely be meeting again before the end of the year. Why piss off Gorbachev? What good would that do? And Reagan wasn't exactly being welcomed with open arms in West Berlin, the part of the city that was supposed to be friendly toward Americans. The day before he was set to arrive, 50,000 leftist protesters took to the streets, blasting Reagan as a warmonger and a promoter of American imperialism. The protesters were met by nearly as many police in riot gear. Much of the capital's Kreuzberg district was placed on lockdown. Somehow the American president who was pushing for freedom and unity for the German people was being portrayed as the enemy of freedom-seeking Germans.

Go figure. Cold War politics could get weird sometimes.

So, what was Reagan going to say when he got there? No one was exactly sure, including White House speechwriter Peter Robinson. In the weeks before Reagan left Washington, Robinson had made an advance trip to Berlin, where he had dinner one night with a group of local citizens, who spent the evening complaining about what a hassle the wall was for them. The city's economy was disrupted. Traffic was a mess. People couldn't visit friends or relatives—or see doctors—on the other side. When he got back to Washington, Robinson produced a speech draft that said explicitly what Reagan had been urging for years: the wall had to go.

Reagan liked what he read, pronouncing it "a nice, solid draft."

But was it too provocative? White House chief of staff Howard Baker thought so. He said the language sounded "unpresidential" and "extreme." People in the State Department shared Baker's concern, fretting that Reagan's harsh words might complicate his continuing efforts to negotiate with Gorbachev. Other White House aides agreed. They pleaded with Reagan to tone down the language. But when he left Washington, no one knew for sure what the president was going to say.

He arrived in Berlin on Air Force One with Nancy at his side. After getting settled, they were driven to the Reichstag, a grand, imposing government building on the left bank of the river Spree that goes back to the Imperial Republic of the late 1800s. From an upper balcony, the Reagans got a bird's-eye view of the wall and the dull expanse of East Berlin behind it. A gray brick sentry and a patrol boat were visible in the distance.

Asked how he felt about the wall, Reagan didn't hesitate: "I think it's an ugly scar."

Asked why some Europeans seemed to believe that Gorbachev was more committed to peace than Reagan was, the American president kept his cool: "They just have to learn, don't they?"

Clearly, he was a man on a mission with a message already in mind.

Reagan delivered his speech the next afternoon outside the Brandenburg Gate, about one hundred yards from the wall. Two sheets of bulletproof glass shielded him from the East Berlin side. Among those in the crowd were West Berlin mayor Eberhard Diepgen and West German chancellor Helmut Kohl. "Tens & tens of thousands of people—stretching as far as I could see," Reagan wrote in his daily diary. Once he got started, there was no turning back. He shoved aside the advice of Howard Baker and the State Department handwringers. He took a full measure of the Cold War and went right at the wall.

"Behind me stands a wall that encircles the free sectors of this city, part of a vast system of barriers that divides the entire continent of Europe," Reagan said, the disdain almost dripping from his voice, setting the stage geographically and philosophically. "From the Baltic south, those barriers cut across Germany in a gash of barbed wire, concrete, dog runs, and guard towers."

He (and Robinson?) took a phrase from President Kennedy, who'd come to Berlin in 1963, two years after the city was divided. "*Ich bin ein Berliner,*" Kennedy famously said that day—literally, "I am a Berliner," meaning, of course, that all of us are. Reagan stuck with English, but he made the same point. "Standing before the Brandenburg Gate," he said, "every man is a German, separated from his fellow men. Every man is a Berliner, forced to look upon a scar." Kennedy's words in Berlin remained one of the best-known speeches from an earlier part of the Cold War. Now, nearly a quarter century later, Reagan was giving voice to how things felt this far in.

By that point in the speech, it was already clear: Reagan was pulling no punches. It was also clear that the Soviet leaders might not like what was coming next.

"In the 1950s," he said, "Khrushchev predicted, 'We will bury you.' But in the West today, we see a free world that has achieved a level of prosperity and well-being unprecedented in all human history. In the communist world, we see failure. Technological backwardness. Declining standards of health. Even want of the most basic kind, too little food. Even today, the Soviet Union still cannot feed itself."

The verdict of history was inescapable, Reagan said. "Freedom leads to prosperity. Freedom replaces the ancient hatreds among the nations with comity and peace. Freedom is the victor."

He made clear exactly which nation was to blame for all this. The Soviet Union. "In Europe, only one nation and those it controls refuse to join the community of freedom. Yet, in this age of redoubled economic growth, of information and innovation, the Soviet Union faces a choice. It must make fundamental changes. Or it will become obsolete."

As he got to that point in the speech, the excitement was rising from the crowd. Bursts of applause were breaking out. The German people were hanging on the American president's every word. He could feel it. He had the audience on his side. As he noted later in his diary, "I got a tremendous reception—interrupted 28 times by cheers." But how far would Reagan go? How explicitly would he address the Soviet leaders? What would he seek from them? Would he name names? How directly would he address the hostile presence of the wall?

He was all in.

"There is one sign the Soviets can make that would be unmistakable, that would advance dramatically the cause of freedom and peace," Reagan said.

And then he got personal. Very personal. "General Secretary Gorbachev," Reagan said, his voice thundering across the dense urban neighborhood, bouncing off that scar of a wall. "If you seek peace, if you seek prosperity for the Soviet Union and Eastern Europe, if you seek liberalization: Come here to this gate! Mr. Gorbachev, open this gate!"

And then the real punch line: "Mr. Gorbachev, tear down this wall!"

Tear. Down. This. Wall.

In the eight years of Reagan's presidency, few words would match the lingering potency of those four. Looking back, it's easy to see why. They embodied everything that people around the world admired about Ronald Reagan. They also embodied everything that others feared. His directness. His firm moral compass. His clarity of vision. His love of freedom. His willingness to go out on a rhetorical limb and express exactly what he was feeling, pushing aside the more cautious voices around him.

Even his ability to predict the future.

The rest of the world would eventually come to recognize that. It would, however, take a little while.

Reagan's Wall speech got some coverage in the media. *Some* coverage. The *New York Times* put it on page 3: "Raze Berlin Wall, Reagan Urges Soviet." But the network newscasts barely noticed, and no one was declaring Reagan's pointed remarks as the start of a new era or the conclusion of an old one or anything like that. No one was predicting when, if ever, the wall was coming down or the Cold War was going to end. The *Time* magazine of Germany, *Der Spiegel*, didn't mention the speech at all, not until months later, then dismissed it as "the work of amateurs." One East German hardliner, speaking on news radio station Deutschlandfunk, tagged Reagan's remarks "an absurd demonstration by a cold warrior." The Soviet press agency Tass reacted just how you'd expect, denouncing the American president's "openly provocative, war-mongering speech."

Clueless, at home and abroad. Who knows? Maybe they'd listened to the Berlin protesters, then skipped the whole speech. But someone else in Moscow was paying close attention, and he didn't seem to mind Reagan's fiery phrasing at all. The primary target. Soviet leader Mikhail Gorbachev. Reagan's summit partner in Geneva, in Reykjavík, and, perhaps in the months to come, in Washington.

No stranger to pointed language himself, Gorbachev made clear that nothing Reagan said remotely perturbed him, no matter what Howard Baker and the anxious State Department crew might have feared. Instead of being put out by Reagan's plea, Gorbachev seemed to accept it for what it was: tough words from an American president who was eager for the Cold War to end. There might even have been some common ground there.

Gorbachev wasn't necessarily embracing Reagan's worldview. Some parts of it he wasn't embracing it all. But at the same time, the Soviet leader wasn't using Reagan's pointed language as an excuse to scuttle their ongoing dialogue. He could have. The fact that he didn't had to mean something. Did it mean that Gorbachev was also ready for the Cold War to end? Reagan hoped so.

Just about a week after the Berlin speech, Reagan was reminded by staff of an imminent U.S. nuclear missile test. The question was whether to give Gorbachev a heads-up. "There was a little difference between Cap & George," the president noted in his diary, meaning Secretary of Defense Caspar Weinberger and Secretary of State George Shultz. "Geo. wants to announce it as in keeping with SALT II treaty which we've said is no longer binding. Cap wants to just go ahead & forget SALT II. On this one I lean toward Geo.— not because of the treaty but because we're on a kind of friendly basis with Soviets leading toward the arms talks."

The president hated to spoil the good feeling . . . *unnecessarily*.

The next few months of 1987 were tense ones for Reagan. Iran-Contra was still raging around him. Black Monday, October 19, brought a 22.6-percent drop in the Dow, the largest one-day tumble in the history of the index. Four days later, the Senate rejected Robert Bork, Reagan's Supreme Court nominee. And some hawkish American conservatives were harrumphing that Reagan and Gorbachev might make some kind of deal limiting short- and medium-range nuclear missiles. Soon, Henry Kissinger, William F. Buckley, even Richard Nixon were piling on. The hawks were mad that MAD might be undermined.

It was a tough time for Gorbachev too. His *perestroika* reforms weren't going smoothly. His hardliners, like Reagan's, were grumbling about the prospect of a missile deal with their nation's fiercest enemy. And one of Gorbachev's strongest and highest-profile supporters, Boris Yeltsin, suddenly turned on him and resigned in protest from the Politburo, something that was almost unheard-of at that level of the Soviet regime. At the same time, Gorbachev was still trying to live down the unfortunate Mathias Rust affair, where a teenage amateur pilot with a nineteen-year-old's idea of how to ease the Cold War flew from Helsinki, Finland, through Moscow's supposedly impenetrable air defense systems and landed untouched on the Bolshoy Moskvoretsky Bridge next to Red Square.

A military analyst named John Pike was looking out the window of the U.S. embassy in Moscow when he saw a small private plane circling over Red Square. "Gee, that's peculiar," Pike remembered thinking. "There's no private aviation in the Soviet Union. Hell, there's no private *anything*." Talk about embarrassing!

The truth was, as their December 8 summit date neared, both Reagan and Gorbachev were in need of a win. And just as Reagan's "Evil Empire" speech didn't rattle Gorbachev when he came into office, the "Tear Down This Wall" speech wasn't rattling the Soviet leader now. If anything, it seemed to focus the Russian, to make him pay attention, to give the summit more urgency, to give both men an extra incentive to get something done.

Would this be the summit that finally produced results? Would the third time for Reagan and Gorbachev be a charm? The signs were encouraging.

Gorbachev and his wife, Raisa, arrived at the White House in style, pulling up in "a limo made in Russia that's bigger than anything we have," Reagan noted. Things got off to a cheery start from there when the two leaders agreed to call each other by their first names. "My first name is Ron," Reagan said, though it's hard to imagine Gorbachev didn't already know that.

"Mine is Mikhail," the Russian leader answered.

"When we're working in private session, we can call each other that," Reagan added, not wanting to take the buddy-buddy thing too far.

But it must have meant something. The two leaders promptly finalized (and signed) the Intermediate-Range Nuclear Forces (INF) Treaty that their aides had been quietly discussing since the last summit, the rumored deal that had Nixon, Kissinger, and William F. Buckley so up in arms. The INF Treaty was major, a genuine reset for U.S.-Soviet arms control. It provided for the dismantling of all—*all!*—Soviet and American medium- and shorter-range missiles. It also established the most extensive system of weapons inspection ever negotiated by the two countries, allowing technicians at sensitive sites on each other's territory for the next ten years.

The two leaders had what White House press secretary Marlin Fitzwater called "a very lively session" on human rights, without making much progress there. There was no give from Gorbachev on Jewish emigration or the other rights issues that Reagan brought up.

Things remained friendly . . . for the most part. Reagan felt comfortable enough with the Russian to write in his diary, "At 10:30 went out to the drive to meet Gorby—(I should say Mikhail)." On the second day of talks they got into some specifics about other missile programs, including Reagan's beloved Strategic Defense Initiative/Star Wars plan. Reagan asked for a certain date when the Soviets would leave Afghanistan. Gorbachev said they'd leave as soon as the U.S. stopped backing the mujahideen, the fierce Islamic militants fighting the Soviet invaders. Wrote Reagan: "I pointed out we couldn't do that unless the puppet govt. laid down their weapons."

The two leaders weren't solving that one. But Reagan, as was his way, hated ending on a sour note. He returned to his friendly, casual approach on the final day when he mentioned, seemingly in passing, Soviet aid to Nicaragua and Vietnamese dominance over Cambodia. "I got him to agree on Nicaragua when he & I took a walk across the lawn," Reagan's diary entry read.

The summit ended with the two most powerful men in the world also agreeing to reduce the total number of strategic ballistic missile warheads to 4,900 each, less than half of what each side was holding. And they agreed to establish a ceiling on the number of sea-launched cruise missiles, something the Russians had been pushing for and the Americans had previously resisted. To get all this done, they sidestepped Reagan's Star Wars dream, which had played such a role in throwing past negotiations off track.

Did this arms control progress foretell the end of the Cold War? Did it make the Berlin Wall come down? Not immediately, in either case. But it sure set a path that would lead to both things being possible in the not-too-distant future, a foundation for the two sides to build on, a trove of trust between two old enemies who finally found some things they could agree on, making the world a safer place.

Reagan termed the summit "a clear success."

"A good deal has been accomplished," Gorbachev agreed.

And none of that happened by accident. It took both of them. Reagan finally had a Soviet counterpart he could do business with, as Britain's Margaret Thatcher had once predicted. And no one was better at face-to-face than Ronald Reagan.

· · ·

Change was unstoppable from there.

The U.S. Senate approved the INF Treaty on May 27, 1988, four months into Reagan's final year in office. Reagan and Gorbachev ratified the treaty five days later, on June 1. Reagan was already out of office when the Berlin Wall finally came down on November 9, 1989, but everyone understood whose words and efforts got that done as the German capital exploded in a massive celebration that included some of the very same protesters who had railed against Reagan's arrival two and a half years earlier.

Historians today call the fall of the wall one of *the* pivotal events of the twentieth century, if not in all of world history, marking the collapse of the figurative Iron Curtain that separated the democratic and communist worlds, ushering in the fall of communism in Eastern and Central Europe and, therefore, ending the Cold War.

That last piece, the official end to the Cold War, occurred just a few weeks after the fall of the wall. Following in Reagan's footsteps, his former vice president, now President George H. W. Bush, met Mikhail Gorbachev in Malta on December 2–3, 1989. There, Bush and Gorbachev declared an official end to the Cold War. After the groundwork that Reagan had laid, it was no big surprise. Still, historians compare the Cold War's formal end to the days after World War II, when British prime minister Winston Churchill, Soviet general secretary Joseph Stalin, and U.S. president Franklin D. Roosevelt met in Yalta and pretty much carved up the world.

Reagan's combined use of the bully pulpit, personal relationships, and adherence to principle is a rare combination today, but it served him once again. Reagan understood that all of those items were necessary to accomplish major goals. He tried to apply that formula to every problem with varying degrees of success—but far more winners than losers.

Thanks to Ronald Reagan, it was a whole new world all over again. Germany was officially reunified in October of 1990.

CHAPTER 18

SO LONG

Leaving the stage is never easy, especially not for someone as accomplished and beloved as Ronald Reagan. Some politicians just slink away. Reagan had a better idea. He showed us how—and why—to say goodbye.

LESSON LEARNED: LEAVE THEM WISHING FOR MORE.

No one lives forever, not even our greatest leaders. *Especially* not our greatest leaders. The human body and the human mind carry on at the pleasure of an invisible alarm clock, which rings on its own schedule, not ours.

So it was for Reagan.

He left the White House on January 20, 1989, every bit as graciously as he came in. He passed the torch to his own vice president, George Bush, who was elected with Reagan's blessing on a Republican platform that promised more of the same.

Every president's dream.

The Reagans moved to a new home in the Bel Air section

of Los Angeles that was purchased for them by several of their wealthy friends, longtime members of the informal kitchen cabinet. The couple later repaid that generosity with the proceeds from speaking fees and book advances. The Ronald Reagan Presidential Library, where I've had the great honor of speaking, opened in Simi Valley in 1991 as a repository of records and a center of discourse and scholarship on ideas that Reagan championed. He mostly kept his distance from day-to-day politics, believing he'd had his turn and others should have theirs. He did address the 1992 Republican National Convention in Houston, though there was so much cheering in the hall it was hard sometimes to make out his words.

"All right, all right . . . ," he kept saying, and "Yes, yes . . ."

"Reagan Back from the Sunset," the *Washington Post* marveled.

The following year, he lent his support to the Brady Handgun Violence Prevention Act, named for White House press secretary James Brady, who was badly wounded the day Reagan was shot. But mostly Reagan was happy to spend his post-presidency seeing longtime friends, working on his memoir, spending time on his ranch outside Santa Barbara, keeping the flame burning with Nancy, and watching old movies on TV. His final speech was on February 3, 1994, at a gala in Washington celebrating his eighty-third birthday. He was his usual grateful self, as if he could hardly believe his lifetime of good fortune.

And then Ronald Reagan went home.

The only time he appeared in public after that was three months later at Richard Nixon's funeral. Time was running out, and he could feel it. That August, he was diagnosed with Alzheimer's disease.

Reagan could have said nothing. His office could have put out a short statement and left it at that. His doctors could have confirmed the diagnosis and then pleaded for privacy. It was *his* life, *his* time, *his* journey. He'd given at the office ... and given and given some more. Truly, he owed nothing to anyone. But Reagan had been writing letters all his life. To friends. To strangers. To people who'd suffered some tragedy. To others celebrating a triumph. To Nancy. He wrote lots of letters to Nancy. Now he had one more letter to write.

"My Fellow Americans," the letter began.

"I have recently been told that I am one of the millions of Americans who will be afflicted with Alzheimer's Disease."

That, right there, was so *Reagan*. Not a drip of self-pity. Not an ounce of false drama. Just a statement of fact, connected to the experiences of countless others, embraced, supported, and openly shared. He was "one of the millions ... ," he said.

The letter was written in Reagan's own hand. It wasn't something Peggy Noonan or Peter Robinson or one of his other speechwriters drafted for him. Every word came from the heart. There's even a big, black scratch-out on the second page, like he was thinking in real time as he was going along.

"Upon learning this news," he continued, "Nancy and I had to decide whether as private citizens we would keep this a private matter or whether we would make this news known in a public way."

Of course, he—and she—were choosing option number two. That's who they were.

"In the past," he noted, "Nancy suffered from breast cancer, and I had my cancer surgeries. We found through our open disclosures, we were able to raise public awareness. We were happy that as a result many more people underwent testing. They were treated in early stages and able to return to normal, healthy lives."

During their time in the White House, the Reagans' openness did quite a bit to raise medical awareness. Both the president and the First Lady revealed they had basal-cell skin cancers removed from their faces. When reporters asked about the tiny bandage on the president's nose, he called it a billboard that said, "Stay out of the sun." In October 1987, Nancy went public with the news that her cancerous left breast was being removed through a mastectomy. Such announcements by public people were far less common back then. There's no doubt her forthrightness helped to drag that disease out of the closet and encouraged other women to go for mammograms. In July of 1985, her husband went public with his own serious health scare when he underwent surgery at Bethesda Naval Hospital to remove a cancerous polyp from his large intestine. Doctors also took out two feet of his lower intestine. The president went in for the exam after getting a call from his brother, Moon, who had just been told he had colon cancer. At seventy-four, Reagan was already America's oldest president.

In that same spirit, he said in the letter, he wanted to share this latest news. "In opening our hearts, we hope this might promote greater awareness of this condition. Perhaps it will encourage a clearer understanding of the individuals and families who are affected by it."

And then he got to the really personal part.

"At the moment I feel just fine," he wrote. "I intend to live the remainder of the years God gives me on this earth doing the things I have always done. I will continue to share life's journey with my beloved Nancy and my family. I plan to enjoy the great outdoors and stay in touch with my friends and supporters.

"Unfortunately, as Alzheimer's Disease progresses, the family often bears a heavy burden. I only wish there was some way I could spare Nancy from this painful experience. When the time comes, I am confident that with your help she will face it with faith and courage."

He had only one last thing to say.

"In closing let me thank you, the American people, for giving me the great honor of allowing me to serve as your President. When the Lord calls me home, whenever that may be, I will leave with the greatest love for this country of ours and eternal optimism for its future.

"I now begin the journey that will lead me into the sunset of my life. I know that for America there will always be a bright dawn ahead."

"The sunset of my life"—that's what he's really talking about and the phrase that lingers most with me. *Here's my life. I've lived it to the best of my ability. I am done.*

To me, what's so great about that letter, besides how truly personal it is, is that Reagan even thought to write it. He could have quietly faded away. He could have left people with the final memories of his presidency or the handful of speeches he delivered afterward. That would have been a fine way to go. But he felt an obligation to say goodbye . . . his way. While he still could, he wanted to make an affirmative gesture to the American people. He wanted to leave on his own terms. Telling people, *I've got this disease. I'm taking it calmly. The time will come that I'm no longer going to know who I am or you are. So before that happens, I want to say goodbye in a way that you will know is in my voice and from my heart and is true to who I am.*

What a courageous decision that was.

Unfortunately, we don't have many leaders like that walking among us today. Ronald Reagan, given a devastating diagnosis, did not think only of himself. Did not engage in self-pity. Today we have leaders like Donald Trump who are in a constant state of grievance. In a constant state of self-pity. At every moment putting himself, his delusions, and, most of all, his self-interest ahead of the people of the country, who honored him with the presidency. It is that selfishness and narcissism that have made our country smaller, angrier, and less successful. Ronald Reagan made us bigger, happier, and historically successful. That is why today, maybe even more than when I cast my first vote in 1980, we must go searching for Reagan. That is why I wrote this book: to remind us what real leadership used to look like. And how great America can be.

Ronald Reagan died at home in Bel Air on June 5, 2004.

His beloved wife, Nancy, died in the same house on March 6, 2016.

The lessons never cease.

EPILOGUE

NO COMPARISON

Where *does* the time go?

It's been three and a half decades since Ronald Reagan delivered his farewell address to the nation and headed off on Air Force One to spend his final years in his adopted home state of California. That's an eternity in government, even longer in politics. Yet, despite the passage of all that time, the lessons of Reagan's life aren't the least bit stale or moldy or irrelevant today. In fact, it seems to me that those lessons are needed even more now than when Reagan held the first inaugural in American history on the west front of the Capitol.

And why did he choose the west front?

Because he wanted to look west. Because he wanted to see the Washington Monument while he was delivering his speech. Because he wanted to see the Lincoln Memorial. Because he wanted to be inspired by great presidents from American history rather than staring at a dreary parking lot and the United States Supreme Court.

By contrast, when Donald Trump stood in that very same spot thirty-six years later, he couldn't see the hope and promise of America. In fact, his squinting eyes conjured up the exact opposite. That day, he spoke darkly of "American carnage" while he railed at enemies, real and imagined. That, right there, is a perfect encapsulation of the many differences between Reagan and Trump.

Reagan saw America's past as an inspiration for an even more hopeful and successful future. Trump gazed into America's past and saw a reminder of the maddening restrictions he thought democracy placed on his authoritarian ambitions. Reagan welcomed "Morning in America." Trump spent his four years in office leading America toward midnight . . . and not the exhilarating midnight of a hopeful New Year's Eve.

His was a dark and foreboding hour from the stormiest depths of a permanent winter.

Trump's cynical vision has now led America to its most divided period in nearly six decades, rivaling even the racial and generational hostility of 1968. Despite inheriting a country that was suffering under Jimmy Carter's double-digit unemployment, double-digit interest rates, and double-digit inflation, Reagan still saw greatness in America's future . . . if we stood by the principles that were laid out by our inspiring leaders of the past. At this divided, self-consumed moment in American history, what we most certainly *don't* need are any more visions of American carnage or a leader who promises that, if given a second term, he'll be our *retribution*.

Retribution: that was a word that never once entered Reagan's White House vocabulary. *Retribution*: it denotes a degree of ugliness Reagan had nowhere inside him.

Though he inherited an economy in ruin, Reagan made the tough decisions to fix it. He cut programs. He supported increased interest rates and did the things that needed to be done to begin to restore America's economy, despite the fact that it led him to a significant drop in his near-term popularity. For his part, Donald Trump promised he would balance the budget in four years and retire the national debt in eight. Rather than take the difficult and unpopular steps needed to implement those promises, he instead *added* $7 trillion to the national debt in four years, the most in any four-year period of the American presidency. Trump left the country nearly $28 trillion in the red, $23,500 in *new* federal debt for every single person in America.

And the visions of the two men were just as starkly different when they turned their attention abroad. When Reagan saw an authoritarian dictator in the Soviet Union, he called Leonid Brezhnev exactly what he was, the leader of an Evil Empire. When Trump saw an authoritarian dictator in former KGB agent Vladimir Putin, he went right to flattery, calling Putin "very savvy . . . a genius . . . very much of a leader." When Reagan saw firsthand the impact of Soviet aggression, he planted himself in Berlin and declared, "Mr. Gorbachev, tear down this wall." When Trump saw the effects of Putin's authoritarian aggression, he signaled his willingness to hand Ukraine to the Russians rather than stand up and fight for freedom, as Reagan did.

When Reagan saw the threat of communism spreading around the world, he routed the Communists from Grenada, he took on the Sandinistas in Nicaragua, and he put unbearable pressure on the rotted foundation of communism in Moscow. In ten years, that led to the collapse of the entire Soviet empire and the dismantling of that hated wall by the free citizens of East *and* West Berlin.

As for Trump, what else did he do when he saw potential for the spread of authoritarian communism around the world? He didn't just suck up to the "genius" Vladimir Putin. He also sent love notes to this "friend" North Korea's Kim Un and said that Xi Jinping, the Chinese despot, was "an exceptionally brilliant individual" straight out of "central casting."

With friends like those, who needs sworn enemies?

So, no, we shouldn't be the least bit surprised that during the Trump administration and its pathetic aftermath (the Biden years) that China's influence would spread, that North Korea's missile technology would advance, that the Russians would pursue a brutal war of aggression in Ukraine, and that Iran would very nearly become a nuclear power.

That's strength versus weakness. Engagement versus isolation. Reagan versus Trump. Reagan constantly standing up to our adversaries, and Trump constantly cozying up to our enemies. On issue after issue, the contrast is just as glaring. When Reagan saw the burden that illegal immigration and a broken immigration system had placed on America, he put his own political popularity at risk by forcing both sides to the negotiating table, producing an admittedly imperfect but certainly better set of immigration laws. And what did Donald Trump do when he was confronted with the next generation of immigration dysfunction? He promised to build a wall the entire length of the U.S.-Mexican border and also promised that Mexico would pay for the wall. Four years later, we had fifty-two miles of new wall and not a single *peso* from Mexico. Even worse, Trump failed to propose any legislative changes to the U.S. immigration system, despite the fact that our party controlled both houses of Congress.

When Ronald Reagan saw a threat to the stability and security of America's Social Security system, he sat down with his own party and with Democrats to craft a Social Security recovery plan. It has served recipients well for the last forty years. When Donald Trump was confronted with a similar crisis and Social Security bankruptcy was little more than a decade away, he chose to ignore it, affirmatively saying the subject was too politically risky for him to take a chance with his own already limited popularity.

When Reagan saw the opportunity to confront the AIDS crisis in America, he acted. Despite his generational misunderstandings about the origins of the virus, he began funding the research that would ultimately lead to life-saving treatments for HIV, turning a swiftly fatal disease into a treatable chronic illness. Compare that with Donald Trump's reaction to the arrival of COVID-19. He unnecessarily shut down our nation's schools, causing harm to students that may take a generation to reverse. He said the virus would disappear on its own or maybe with the injection of sunlight or bleach into people's bodies. While he did fund Operation Warp Speed to develop a vaccine, he moaned incessantly about the impact the pandemic was having on his beautiful economy and spent little or no time expressing compassion for the victims and their families as the death toll quickly surpassed 1 million.

The American people got all this . . . and responded accordingly. Just look at the two different ways the voters responded when these two presidents offered themselves for reelection. As Ronald

Reagan campaigned for a second term in 1994, it truly was "Morning in America." Interest rates, inflation, and unemployment were all back to single digits. America was experiencing the largest economic boom since the years immediately after World War II. This was a country that once again believed that its tomorrow could be better than its yesterday. And so the people rewarded the leader who made that possible: a reelection victory in forty-nine of the fifty states for Ronald Reagan, a resounding affirmation of both the man and the lessons he taught.

Donald Trump ran a reelection campaign of more anger, bitterness, and division, highlighted by a one-on-one debate where he managed to interrupt his opponent seventy-three times in ninety minutes, leaving the country even more divided, dispirited, and dysfunctional than before. Their verdict on his stewardship? An electoral defeat by a man who had tried for the presidency three times before and had never won a race outside the state of Delaware and only 232 electoral votes for Trump, far short of the 270 needed to secure his reelection. That was less than half the 525 electoral votes the American people gave to Ronald Reagan as his reward for a job well done.

And now?

Amazingly, some elements of the Republican Party are willing to consider going "Back to the Future" with Donald Trump. Only this version of that Reagan-era movie won't be nearly as fun as Michael J. Fox's gleeful time machine adventure or even Reagan's portrayal of George Gipp in *Knute Rockne All American*. It threatens instead to be far closer to Jack Torrance, the maniacal character Jack Nicholson portrayed in *The Shining*.

"Here's Johnny!"

No. Please, no.

Some people might wonder what I consider the true essence of the difference between Ronald Reagan and Donald Trump. Is it just that Reagan was born into poor circumstances in a strained family in the middle of the country and that Donald Trump was born to a wealthy, unified family in the largest metropolis in the United States? I'm sure that provides some contribution to their differences. But the biggest difference is not geography or wealth or upbringing. The biggest difference between them, I'm convinced, is one simple but extraordinarily powerful word.

Character.

Ronald Reagan had it. Donald Trump does not.

Reagan believed that a man's word was his bond. Trump believes his word on any issue is just a temporary inconvenience. Reagan believed that America was at its best when it was generous to others in both our gifts and our example. Trump believes America is at its best when it is looking out only for itself and, most particularly, only for him as its exalted leader.

Reagan believed that the way you leave the world after you've been given the opportunity to lead is the best proof of who you are as a man and a president. Trump thought the only measure of his success or failure was whether or not he was reelected. And when he wasn't, he was willing to lie to the American people to give himself that false affirmation of a result he could not achieve. Once again, Reagan was right.

Look at the America he handed to George H. W. Bush in January of 1989. A country unified and prosperous and a world about to be free from communism and the Iron Curtain about to be lifted. And Reagan watched as power passed seamlessly from his hands through the hands of his chosen successor, carrying on a tradition that went all the way to the earliest days of America.

The country Donald Trump left to Joe Biden was scarred by the violence the outgoing president incited on January 6, divided by his claims of a stolen election, and commemorated with an inauguration conducted behind fencing to try to deter a second attack in two weeks on the Capitol of the United States.

Did Trump watch from the steps of the Capitol as power was once again peacefully transferred to a new president? Of course not. He skipped the inauguration entirely, the first president to diss his successor that way since Andrew Johnson, who was also the first president to be impeached. As his successor was sworn in, Trump was holding his breath and spewing complaints as he flew one last time on Air Force One, bound for Florida, where he promptly began undercutting the country he had the honor of leading for the previous four years.

The reason I wrote this book and titled it *What Would Reagan Do?* is that our party and our country both need to return to the values that Reagan's life and career taught us. The lessons are right there for the learning. That in America, winning is not a zero-sum game. That all Americans can do well when we stand strong for the things we believe in, listen to each other about our differences, make solving our country's problems our first priority, and understand that the world is a better place when America leads and doesn't hide.

Times keep changing, but Reagan lives on.

ACKNOWLEDGMENTS

Writing a book, you have so many people to thank for your ability to place it into the world. This effort is no different.

Many thanks for their inspiration every day to my four wonderful children: Andrew, Sarah, Patrick, and Bridget.

My dad is a regular source of support, and his mind and spirit are indefatigable. At ninety years old, he serves as a role model every day.

Special thanks to my brother, Todd, who always encourages me and stands by me during all of life's challenges and triumphs.

This book is my third project with my literary soul brother, Ellis Henican. After *Let Me Finish*, *Republican Rescue*, and now this book, we have a very special friendship and a very easy collaboration. Ellis is a first-class talent. This book would not have ever been completed without his boundless intellectual curiosity and top-notch work ethic. Once again, he made this experience a very special journey.

My agents at WME have once again given me great guidance and wise representation. The incomparable Mel Berger as my literary agent took the concept of this book and quickly turned it into a reality. The team at WME continues to present me with new challenges and opportunities along with a defined path on how to get these projects done.

Natasha Simons, my editor at Simon & Schuster, provided real input and focus to our effort. She loves Ronald Reagan and challenged us to make this book reach its potential. I think she succeeded.

Roberta Teer has once again played the role of researcher extraordinaire. She makes sure that the facts that Ellis and I are absolutely sure of actually *are* facts! Thanks once again to her.

Writing this book while also preparing to run for president of the United States requires real discipline and real support from your team. My greatest respect and thanks go out to Bill Palatucci, Maria Comella, Mike DuHaime, Russ Schriefer, Cam Henderson, Collin Cummings, Douglass Mayer, Jordan Riggs, Karl Rickett, Joe Ahearn, Brandi Marks, Nicole Ossola, Michele Brown, Lauren Fritts, Rich Bagger, Bob Grady, Bob Martin, Foster Morss, and Brian Jones.

Finally, thanks to Ronald Wilson Reagan, the fortieth president of the United States and the first person I ever voted for in a presidential election. He has always served as a role model. I hope we can return our country to the type of politics practiced by President Reagan.